A YEAR IN A SMALL COUNTRY

A Year in a
Small Country

Edited by
Jon Gower

First Impression—1999

© Jon Gower, Patrick Dobbs, Christine Evans,
and William Condry's estate.

© illustrations: Chris Neale

ISBN 1 85902 646 X

*Printed in Wales at
Gomer Press, Llandysul, Ceredigion*

Contents

Introduction

. . . and so the days drift on like leaves—like the leaves of a book which keep the secrets and revelations of the day, or the crimped and crenellated leaves that blanket a forest floor. And with that drift, that inexorable move towards shortest day then back to lengthening light, the passage of the seasons takes us with it to an understanding, about the restorations of spring and the laziness of summer—and on to the beneficence of autumn and the challenge of winter . . .

Diarists, like dormice, are scarce and precious. The pace of modern life, lived at a lick, seems to allow too little time for recording and contemplation, especially at day's end, with too much tomorrow to prepare for. Fewer diary keepers now chart the quotidian changes that together make up the rhythm of the march of seasons. Much as contemporary poetry turns increasingly urban, concerned with the inner spiritual and emotional geography of poets rather than with the world of nature, thus making the nature poet a scarcer thing, so too, perhaps is the nature diarist a threatened species. Yet there still remains a small space in the broadsheet papers for wildlife diaries, bringing news of swallows' return and stoats in ermine, for chance encounters and floral delights. This book brings together three diarists—a naturalist, a hill farmer and a poet—a trio of relationships with the land and animals, three sensibilities in different registers. The late William Condry notes nature's ebbs and flows around his home set in the marshlands of the Dyfi estuary during 1996. We can compare the 1997 diaries of Carmarthenshire sheep farmer and writer Patrick Dobbs— writing at a time when agriculture was settling deeper into the doldrums—and poet Christine Evans, vacillating between Bardsey island and her mainland home on the Llŷn peninsula.

William Condry was the doyen of Welsh naturalists, a quietly spoken and genuinely humbling man, whose voice in prose was as soft as in life whilst always remaining authoritative. His gentleness is evident in the diary accounts for *A Year in a Small Country*, such as that of the day he managed, with infinite calm, to stroke an adder's head, or the time he calmly observed a woodmouse chewing his fingernail.

I first came across him as the author of the magisterial *Natural History of Wales* in the Collins New Naturalist series, a rich repository of fact and anecdote in which I, as a schoolboy, learned that avalanches weren't confined to the Alps. The one in Llandrillo in 1895 'rushed down the very steep hillside carrying all before it: walls, hedges and anything movable.' The book is a lapidary of such gems, from the folklore of cloudberries to the history of the Welsh clearwing moth. He is alert to language, even if his own is never showy: the name of the high moorland of the Migneint is to Welsh ears, he suggests 'squelchy with suggestions of boggy hollows'.

Bill was a regular contributor to *The Guardian*'s Saturday country diary, a window which had been allowing readers a glimpse of the countryside since 1906. Bill started contributing in 1957, although he himself had kept a journal since 1927, bringing news of white-fronted geese scything through winter skies above his home, and of mountain walks which took him to discover alpine flowers anchored in the rocks, sometimes the self-same species that the pioneering naturalist Edward Llwyd would have chanced upon three centuries previously. A visit to Ynys Edwin, the house he shared with his wife Penny—where they moved to live for 'a touch of wildness and the company of ravens'—would always invariably be blessed by some serendipitous sighting: a pied flycatcher newly returned from Africa, the male resplendent in black and white plumage as if it were ready for a dinner party, or thrushes creating a chamber piece in the middle of oak woodlands. But the most uplifting sighting would be Bill and Penny themselves, usually at work within their *horus conclusus*, a walled garden which benefitted from twenty green fingers and an interest in plant hunting, the pair of them all smiles and secateurs.

In their quiet stone house, through a kitchen seemingly always wreathed in the aroma of fresh bake, you entered the living room which danced with light refracted through the leaves outside. The coffee table groaned with magazines showing the range of Bill's conservation interests, whilst the bookshelves reflected the man's interests in biographies and autobiographies, especially about the natural history and exploration of Africa. To read his diaries is to visit again that three-hundred-year-old house in the middle of a nature reserve and be surprised by a wisp of snipe or a spring of teal in the marsh that led to their outbuildings. It is to hear that gentleness again.

Anyone who knew about Bill's interest in the American naturalist Henry Thoreau might look for comparisons between his home south of Machynlleth and Thoreau's Walden Pond. It was another great naturalist, R. M. Lockley, who commissioned Bill Condry to write a book about Thoreau for the Great Naturalists series, having remembered that Bill slept with a copy under his pillow. Bill was a contemplative naturalist, certainly not a materialistic man, and a bit of a pantheist, not that he'd have allowed such a label without a debate. One of his great friends was the poet R. S. Thomas, perhaps the greatest pantheist poet of the century and in my mind's eye I can see them now, walking with purpose up the screes of Snowdonia, climbing higher now where choughs are tossed through the air like flakes of ash from a bonfire and there are tiny blurts of colour among the rocks, saxifrages and stonecrops, rockroses and perfect gentians. The two of them often walked the hills and mountains and it is one of my greatest regrets that I never took up their offer to join them on one of their walks.

Bill was a wise man who taught me, for one, that wild Wales is a thing of the past and that man's influence—rapacious rather than benign—has changed the landscape unutterably. This was something he learned during his childhood as he realised that the great and overemployed tarmac gang of the twentieth century was about to swallow up the countryside around his home, burying the ancient kingdom of Mercia. The lapwings stopped flying like black and white butterflies, the rasping cry of the corncrake—so much like two big wooden spoons being rasped against each other—was no longer heard and the larks simply stopped ascending. This kindled a flame of righteous anger which flickered to life every now and then in his writings, a man angered by the spread of alien conifers, the creation of ugly reservoirs and in fear of the exploding human population. But he also felt blessed by the abundance of wildlife remaining in Wales, a genuine joy which dances under the surface in books such as *Wildlife, My Life* and *Pathway to the Wild*.

A keener botanist than birdwatcher, Bill could read the land beneath from the flora which clothed its surface and it is no coincidence that one of the books he finished before his death was a biography of the indefatigable Dolgellau botanist Mary Richards. There is ample evidence that he could occasionally put humankind itself under the microscope, though often his overriding sense was of the great sweep of geological time, such as the day he found himself on the top of Tryfan, 'where it was good to be up there treading the grey carpet of woolly-haired moss among the debris of yesterday's world and thinking about the slow forces that have shaped the earth, and will go on shaping it long after the trivial human incident is over'.

It is now twenty years since Christine Evans penned her first poem, written at a time when she was living with her infant son and fisherman husband in the small community on Bardsey island, Ynys Enlli, one of the last toe-holds of a traditional culture in Wales. Her husband Ernest is one of the island's children.

Christine 'was struck most by Enlli's patterns, the invisible web of relationships and deferential conventions that held the community together, and the way it remains a relatively frugal way of life, crofting rather than farming, on a handful of small, salt-scorched fields.' Christine divides her time between life on the island and Uwchmynydd, above-the-mountain, which is only 600 feet above sea-level but which gains in stature by its proximity to the sea and to the brontosaurus hump of island which lies across the fast-racing sound.

Her relationship with the island might perhaps have been prefigured by one of her father's early gifts. When Christine was eight he gave her a copy of *Early Morning Island* by that pioneering naturalist and prolific writer R. M. Lockley. Her father had bought it on a bookstall in Manchester. Lockley's descriptions of life on the Pembrokeshire islands must have cast its gentle spell on this writer, as they did on so many people.

Life on Bardsey is not always idyllic. Christine feels that 'sometimes it's a sanctuary and sometimes it's a prison' and in that she echoes directly another writer who took the island as her theme and home, the artist Brenda Chamberlain, whose *Tide Race* tells how tough and testing the island of twenty thousand saints can be, whilst being also kissed by blessedness.

Christine was brought up by her Welsh grandmother until she was 18 months old and imagines that her first words might have been Welsh. The seeds of her empathy with Wales were planted early and planted deep.

For many years she was a teacher of English in Pwllheli and there were times when she felt guilty about the fact that she was making pupils see English as an attractive medium for personal expression at a time when the Welsh syllabus was still rather starchy and academic.

Christine was born in West Yorkshire and educated at the University of Exeter but came to Pwllheli, her father's birthplace, to teach English in 1967. She has published four volumes of poetry starting with *Looking Inland*, described as observations of the 'rural communities of Llŷn with a mature perception and profound sympathy.'

The geography of *Looking Inland* is to be found on the cover, a map of the western edge of the Llŷn peninsula and, offshore, *Ynys Enlli*, beatific Bardsey. There are some poems shot through with the simple glory of poetic unexpectedness, such as 'Winter Digging', reminiscent of Seamus Heaney's—not surprising perhaps when she lists Heaney along with David Constantine on her list of favourite poets, sitting alongside women prose-writers such as Helen Dunmore, Carole Shields, Margaret Atwood, Alice Hoffman and Sylvia Plath:

> But a raven croaks above me, a black
> defiance in the sky; a curlew, close, unchains
> his syllables like confident balloons
> and the grazing ewes
> of cumulus are stirred
> miles high, docile to
> momentousness I cannot feel.

Falling Back (The Shepherd's Widow) which followed in 1985 is a meditation on grief, the story of a young woman dealing with the death of her husband. This was followed by *Cometary Phases* in 1989 which won a Welsh Arts Council Prize. It is a long poem in seven sections, each springing from an attempt to catch a sighting of Halley's Comet in 1986, and addressed to Christine's son who was determined to see it 'next time round', working out that he'd be 87 at the time.

There are poems which scrutinise and celebrate middle age, poems of a gifted insomniac, and anthropomorphic fantasies in which the poet becomes, variously, a whale, a tree-wife, and an owl. The latter underlines Christine's shivery lyricisms when describing nature. But this is no romantic wishy-washiness. This is nature red in blood and claw as a spider advances on its prey:

> The wide gape of my legs
> longs to enfold and mould what is mine
> soothe its spasms in a shroud of silk
> stroke it into succulence
> love it until it is all juice.

Christine's latest volume is a paean of praise to enchanted Enlli, the Insula Sanctorum, once known fancifully as the 'Rome of Britain.' Talking to Christine you can hear the faint quiver of excitement in her voice as she describes her recent investigations into the island's natural history: she is 'getting down to my neglected education. I used to feel that it wasn't important what things are called.' This past summer she has been getting into geology, learning from an MSc student engaged in studies involving surveying water. This suits her much more than birdwatching—even though Bardsey is a landing stage for many migrants and home to huge colonies of seabirds. There's a simple reason for this. 'I don't see well and the birds don't stay still long enough.' Turning naturalist is logical enough a step for a poet who is so finely attuned to the natural world. Anyone who's read some of her Bardsey poems knows her ability to get to the essence of a thing—'snails, fat wall fruit, creep and chuckle' and 'nine oystercatchers, three groups of three/past past, printed on the sky's pigeon breast/like a logo, even their cries symmetrical.' There are 'seals with faces of grave elders' and 'swarms of jellyfish drift in the Cafn, pulsing slowly/like gas mantles, translucent parachutes of intelligence,' and in the more human world 'roof slates gleam with the bloom of ripening plums.' There are also marvellous lists. In the poem 'Broc Môr' tidedrifted items are inventoried, serendipitous surprises come to shore, from a 'barrel bursting with butter sweating salt' to the 'Japanese mask/that hung by the fire to send Tŷ Pella kids/shrieking to bed' and 'Arthur's clogs, the left/picked up in March, its match two months later.' As one might expect in an island collection there are ample references and the occasional poem about weather, with one, 'Through the Weather Window' veritably lurching and tossing with the swell of the waves. It took me back to Bardsey, where I spent my most idyllic summer, even if the journeys to Porth Meudwy and Aberdaron were hardly blessed by millpond calm:

> The boat rolls, and dips, and rises
> as the ocean's grey skin heaves.
> Green troughs yawn, folded ventricles
> sliced to the aortic quick
> to the mineral veins
> of cobalt, emerald and viridian
> running fast, nudged over
> to pulse and burst again.

There is a quotation on the living room wall of Patrick Dobbs' Carmarthenshire farmhouse. It comes from Book II, the King of Brobdingnag section of *Gulliver's Travels* and reads 'And he gave it for his opinion that whosoever could make two blades of corn or two blades of grass to grow where only one had grown before would deserve better of mankind and do more essential service to his country than the whole race of politicians put together.'

Patrick is a sheep farmer and writer who pens more than a few sheep in a gap of cloud in Llanddeusant. He has also tried his hand at politics having stood as a Labour candidate for Leominster in 1979. Blaenau Farm—which means and stands at the head of a valley—is set where the land rises towards Llyn y Fan with its legendary maiden and the great sweep of the

Carmarthen Van with its rockroses amid ravens. The farm sits at 850 ft above sea level with Patrick's grazing going up to 2650 ft at the summit of *Bannau Sir Gâr*.

Patrick has eighty seven acres in the fence, along with common grazing on the Black mountains but his sheep are also to be found grazing from Cardigan Bay to Salisbury plain. He cautiously admits he has several hundred, almost all being Welsh mountain sheep with a few crossed with Cheviots. On his boundary is the old farmstead of Gellionnen, still surrounded by ash trees. 'I know that last family to farm there. Now it belongs to someone from England. There are too many such properties in Llanddeusant.' Maintaining his boundary isn't easy. Patrick once wrote: 'For thirty years I have maintained a mountain fence alongside the largest, and perhaps one of the most heavily grazed, commons in Europe. How many stakes have I carried up the mountainside in burning sun or wild north-east wind! How many times have I smashed a crevice in the rock with an iron crowbar to make a post secure come drought or blizzard!'

His childhood was spent in a good many places—the Cotswolds, Birmingham, Oxford and north Wales. On a tube ride in London he read an advertisement which proclaimed, 'He who plants a fine avenue of trees cannot in the nature of things hope to enjoy them in their glory.' That sentiment must have lodged quite deeply, for one of Patrick's great joys on the farm is his 'avenue of ten conker trees—horse chestnuts—on one side of the road to Llyn y Fan. After we're dead and God help us forgotten there'll be people who'll be thankful for it.' Patrick is going to be buried at Blaenau, has made the necessary plans already. 'If I die in the winter I want to be buried in the plantation of trees.' Should he die in the summer he'll be buried higher up on the farm, above waterworks' cottage. He reckons that winter would make things difficult—'probably the wheels of the tractor would slip.' He has, in addition to the horse chestnuts, planted a veritable arboretum of native trees—wild cherries, crabapples, rowan, oak, ash and birch.

Patrick moved to Blaenau farm, with its 'cold, wet, old stone house' on April Fool's Day, 1961. An earlier wanderlust had seen him undergoing a four-week sea voyage which took him to spend a period during 1959-60 in British Guyana as it was then called. There he worked on the Leonora plantation owned by Sandbach Parker, a poor relation of Booker Brothers and McConnell whose descendant company sponsors the nowadays tarnished prize for fiction. The plantation sat on the estuary of the Demerara and Essequibo rivers, a jungly place which was really part of the Amazon basin. Patrick explains, 'If we hadn't grown sugar there it would have been rain forest. It was extremely hot, very, very colourful with tremendous animals, birds, fish and plants. I loved the forest, loved the quietness, loved the complete absence of traffic. There were no roads and we had to move about by river using dug-out canoes. I loved the Amerindians whom we called "bucks" and the people on the plantations too who were very good-humoured despite their living tough lives and fairly short ones.'

Before that Patrick had worked in Canada—on a cattle ranch, in a feed mill and in the stock yards in 1957-58, this just after completing a degree in agriculture at Wye College, University of London.

His first success at writing came when he was ten years of age when he wrote a poem about going uphill which won half a guinea in a competition in the *Mickey Mouse* comic—an august organ 'which was for kids who hadn't graduated to the *Beano* and the *Dandy*.' Patrick cites this ten and sixpence as being, pro rata, the most he's ever received for a published poem.

Over the years he has been published in *Farmers' Weekly*, *The Countryman*, *Country Life* and *Punch* although many of his poems only exist in his head. He performs with great exuberance of spirit, as anyone who has witnessed his spirited and flambuoyant performances at the poems and pints sessions of the annual gatherings of the Welsh Union of Writers will attest. These take you a bit by surprise because he is such a quiet man, diffident sometimes, but possessed of strong opinions on certain things, as befits a farmer with a hard hill life.

In 1990, having been awarded the John Morgan prize, Patrick took an old suitcase—a relic from an itinerant youth—and an ancient brown briefcase he'd bought at a charity sale and headed for Ireland. There he bought a second-hand bicycle on the Donegal side of Londonderry and set off to ride the debatable ground of the Northern Ireland border.

He took a tape recorder with him but the device proved inhibiting, so Patrick restored to note-taking. But taking notes in troubled times can be dangerous. So Patrick invented a code which even the most accomplished code breaker would find a puzzler. He kept a record in Welsh of what he saw and heard but using characters from the Greek alphabet!

On his journey he noticed changes in agriculture since his earlier visits to Ireland in the late 1940s and 1950s. One was the absence of horses . . . 'I missed them. I have always found something companionable about a horse, for which tractors have proved to be a noisy, oily and expensive substitute. If agriculture had been the merchanised business it has now become when I first went to work on a farm I think I would have tried something else.' On his bicycle tour he noticed other farming features which reminded him of his own way of working. He saw a poor farmer spreading muck by hand with a dung fork. 'I had thought I was the last man in Western Europe to go in for that particular chore.' In the corner of a field he saw a small haystack thatched with rushes which 'offered a small window on a bit of my own history that I thought I had forgotten' because 'as a young farmworker in Devon in the 1950s I did believe that I was the last man in England to thatch a haystack. I scythed my own bundle of reed and cleft my own spars of hazel.'

Here for a Month also found Patrick in the town of Middletown, a formerly busy railway junction where the railway had gone. It put him in mind of other towns he had visited during a life in which he has been many things—colt-breaker, sheep-shearer, farrier and mill-hand.

'I remembered a town in the Rocky Mountains of Western Canada . . . the mine had closed and the people had walked away, leaving the streets and their homes to the elk, the moose and the grizzly bears. And I remember the mining settlement of Saint Peter's, lost in the tropical rain forests of Guyana, where the machinery had been stripped by a scrap dealer from Cardiff to be taken back across the Atlantic, reputedly in the last commercial voyage of a square-rigged sailing ship. Only a few buckets and shovels remain behind.'

The many threats to agriculture, and the genuine rural crisis that grips our land, might well mean that there will be fewer men like Patrick on the hills of Wales in the future. It would be a loss too profound for words.

JANUARY

The Otter / *Y Dwrgi*

Otters are the Scarlet Pimpernels of the riverbank, much sought after but so elusive that a sighting is a champagne moment. A very engaging book about otters by a great enthusiast, Paul Chanin, tongue wedged firmly in cheek, maintained that, armed with a distribution map, one ought to be able to see otters. He reckoned that, 'In most areas where otters are doing well, a fortnight of waiting twenty-four hours a day should normally be enough.' You stand as much of a chance in the bleak midwinter, when otter tracks are a surefire signature that they've been and gone, as you do in summer, when cubs add to the general waterside and underwatery activities. Truth be told, though I have searched for them in all months, and all over Wales, I have only seen otters on two occasions. My first sighting was on a January day, at the confluence of the rivers Mochdre and Severn in Mid Wales—a brief Loch Ness Monster-style hump breaking a pane of water between two riffles. That's why the otter appears in this month—and the chances of seeing otters in January are on a par with July. My real red letter day for otters came when I saw five on a spring morning.

Imagine the mock enthusiasm set into the faces of a small and bleary film crew getting up slightly before the sun and walking out to the ponds at Stackpole in Pembrokeshire. To film otters? How could you film them if you couldn't bloody well see them? That sort of enthusiasm.

The Countryside Council of Wales warden, a genial and most knowledgeable man, Bob Haycock, was in a genuinely optimistic mood as was 'Mr Otter', also known as Geoff Lisles from the Welsh Otter Trust. Geoff's luck has changed in recent years. He sees otters nowadays: there had been a long, fallow period when he'd been studying them without seeing any at all.

The wind sussurated through the reeds—tall stands of Phragmites—as I looked for pike near a sluice where a monster specimen had been recently sighted, reminding myself, as I peered into the depths, of some lines by the Welsh poet Duncan

Bush. He describes pike perfectly as having 'the neurasthenic grin of the Hollywood killer.' I failed to spot one of Izaak Walton's 'freshwater wolves', and so far no otters were spotted either, although they had been reported on a pond which is separated from the surf of St. Brides' bay by a shingle bank. Apparently otters have even been seen in the sea hereabouts— uncommon behaviour, to say the least, around the Welsh coast, although it is quite common in otter haunts in Scotland.

Suddenly, there they were, gambolling and porpoising— aquanautic in the same way as, say, a peregrine falcon is aeronautic; Pembrokeshire torpedoes, homing in on a fresh fish breakfast! Underwater, the otter's eyes, which have lenses that can be modified in shape, allow it to compensate for refraction in the water. In murkier places, the long whiskers, sensitive to vibrations, help it to find its food. It enjoys eels above all others, perhaps because they are slower, thus easier to catch, but trout and sticklebacks, roach and perch also feature on the otter's list of favourite fish. We were even fortunate enough to see one pass underwater, sleekly and sinuously, as we crossed a wooden walkway over one of the lily ponds. The glimpse was enough to see why the otter is an underwater angler par excellence, its body scything through the weeds. Their high whistles might have summoned old fashioned policemen, peelers or bobbies, from their beat. This wasn't just luck, but great ladlesful of it.

Otters are underwater weasels, members of the muscelid family and are to be found across a geographical range which stretches from the west of Ireland to the northern rim of Africa, from the tropical rainforests of Asia to the freezing arctic tracts of Finland.

That afternoon Geoff Lisles took me looking for evidence of otters along a stretch of river leading away from the deep cleft in the rock which is the Cilgerran Gorge. We found spraints, or droppings, and saw otter resting places and tracks through the grass where the otters' long thin bodies and short legs prove ideally suited for pushing their way through. Some paths were very well worn, otters being creatures of habit, and some of the resting places have been recorded as being in use for periods of

4

up to forty years. I wasn't too keen to follow Geoff's words of encouragement and roll the spraints around between thumb and forefinger but this released a not unpleasant musky smell which marks them out from scats, the droppings of mink, which stink.

Some Welsh otters have proved themselves to have good heads for heights, with one spraint site being ten foot up a tree near the river Wye. Despite the sweet smell of their droppings I still wouldn't like to be caught under such a tree!

We also saw a few tracks, the prints in soft mud showing clearly that an otter has five toes, unlike cats and dogs which have four.

Which all goes to prove that with serendipity on your side, and a couple of experts to hand, you ought to be able to see an otter, now happily spreading in Wales, though still a denizen of a world invisible to most. It's a fine creature, this underwater mammal. To see one is a beatitude of bright water.

William Condry

The year began well. We had days of zephyr and mildness and on the 13th the first great tit sang his ringing notes. On the 18th, cutting bracken for garden mulching, I heard a red kite calling in the upper airs and for nearly half an hour he circled over the oakwood, calling beautifully. I was astonished. At any season, and especially in the heart of winter, kites have very little to say to the world and I still wonder what this rare demonstration was all about. That same day the lesser spotted woodpecker came into 'song' if that is a correct description of its muted, kestrel-like squeaking. Year after year, with commendable punctuality, this is the date (give or take a day or two), when we first hear him calling or drumming, provided the weather is fairly kind.

Things began to change on January 19. At first all was windstill, mild and bright. But after lunch a biting east wind suddenly burst upon us bringing inspissated gloom. It blew for days and, as usual in such weather, our western woods filled with woodcocks driven out of the north by snow. Then it was our turn to have a covering of snow and by the 29th our estuary, the Dyfi, was partly frozen—a rare event.

By the end of the month, though the wind was still bitter, the real sting had gone out of it and there came a day to remember. It was all to do with horses and what long necks they have. Although our garden hedge is more or less protected by barbed wire, it gets savaged most winters when the horses are at their hungriest. So I decided to make the fence higher and as I worked I was closely observed by ten inquisitive horses. Suddenly two of them went galloping off into some long grass a hundred yards away. There, to my surprise, they flushed a large brown bird. As it flew towards me I thought it was a tawny owl but then it turned sideways and I could see it had a long neck and was in fact a bittern. These days the bittern is more than a rare bird: it is a symbol of a lost world. Centuries ago the booming of bitterns, said to be the loudest of all bird sounds, was an everyday noise. *Aderyn y bwn*, the booming bird, was known throughout Wales. What a picture that gives us of the vast swamps and reed-beds of former days!

* * *

Lately in Gwent, in search of ancient things, I came to Skenfrith and it's a gem of a medieval castle at the side of the Monnow stream. As Skenfrith is only half a mile into Wales from Herefordshire, I had assumed that the name was an English import. Not so: it is a badly mangled form of its Welsh name, Ynysgynwraidd. There are many such contortions in Wales. In Gower, Oystermouth represents a despairing effort to get the English tongue around Ystumllwynarth. Elsewhere in Glamorgan, Coytrahene may look exotic until you realise it was once Goetre Hen. Coldbrook in Gwent should not be taken at its face value: it is simply a version of Colbrwg. So the catalogue goes on. Llanbedr gets enfeebled into Lampeter; Caerdydd degenerates into Cardiff; Brycheiniog shrinks to Brecon. Crickhowell is strictly Crucywel; Kidwelly is Cydweli; Ludchurch is really Eglwys Lwyd; Landore is disguise for Glandŵr. In north Wales is the River Wheeler; but trace it to its source, etymologically speaking, and you find the Welsh name Chwiler. In Anglesey I recall the bizarre name Quirt: I suppose it was originally Cwrt. Not only Welsh names got corrupted. In Gwent in the Middle Ages there was a priory known as Parc Grace Dieu. It ended up as Parkers Due!

Place names can be fun and people have been enjoying them ever since the Dark Ages when it was part of the stock in trade of story tellers to explain strange place names through fictitious inventions. The Roman road name, Sarn Helen, seems likely to have come from Sarn (a road, especially a metalled road) plus some word like Leon (as in Caerleon), from the Latin *Legionum*, 'of the Legions'. But our story tellers had other ideas. For them Sarn y Leon was the Sarn of Elen or Helen and they supported the idea with lovely yarns about this Helen who was described as the Welsh wife of a Roman emperor. They even had her intervening with him on behalf of the people of Wales, persuading him to improve the road system. So one of the great Welsh roads got the name Sarn Helen; and Helen has been with us ever since. (See the *Mabinogion* story: 'The Dream of Macsen Wledig').

Patrick Dobbs

It is the first of January 1997 and it is very cold. The east wind brings with it a dusting of powdery snow which piles up in the shelter of every rock and tussock. It squirms and squeezes its way through the gaps and holes in the walls and the roofs and the stones and slates and the doors and the windows. The hay-bales at the top of the stack are iced like a Christmas cake, the cattle are sprinkled white as a sugared plum pudding and even the dogs in their shelters don't entirely escape.

The ground beneath is hard, for we have had almost continual frost since before Christmas. The sheep are still on the mountain, and although the cold is intense and the snow blowing they are safe enough for a time. But for how long a time? If the white flakes thicken and the fall becomes heavy they will be difficult to move through the drifts; they won't know where to look for their next mouthful and they may even get buried.

I wrap up warm, with no chinks in my layers of protective clothing. I hang my whistle round my neck, pull gloves (Gloves! It must be cold!) on to my hands and lock the front door against the storm. A flick on the bolt to their run and Jess and Bob rush out to join me, delighted at the prospect of the day ahead.

Old Wimpole, retired these many years, hardly hears us depart. Nell is heavily pregnant as usual and Solo rests for another day. Although I generally gather my more distant sheep on horseback there can be no question of riding today, for the ground will be far too unpredictable and unyielding beneath my horse's feet and my perch impossibly cold on top of his back.

Once over the slippery and treacherous bars of the cattle grid beside the mountain gate, I follow the bank of Nant Melyn and turn up Fan Foel towards the source of the Usk. I can see nothing but swirling snow, and hear nothing over the howl of the gale. No sheep, no horizon, no view, no birds fly and no jets scream overhead. Threescore winters, and one or two more beside, have already besieged my brow, and I wonder how long I can go on doing this. The going beneath is firm and hard and the snow cover thin, but it is still a tough climb up Pantygwin's walk. But so much of my working life, and of my playtime too, has been spent on horseback that I take comfort from the thought that Allah does not count to a man the years spent in the saddle. No sheep are sheltering in the peat and heather beside the river, or if they are I can't see them, and I'm not crossing into Breconshire this morning for I aim to clear the Myddfai mountain before nightfall.

If I was a musical man I suppose I would hum a tune or whistle the latest from Radio Two. But I know my limitations, I can't whistle, and have always stuck to a piece of advice I picked up from Michael Foot at a Labour party meeting in Brecon—'When in Wales, never sing.' So I declaim poetry instead, starting with the twenty-third psalm,

'The Lord is my shepherd . . .'

through Eskimo Nell,

'. . . A moose or two, a caribou,
A bison cow or so. . .'

a few *hen benillion*,

'*Ni chawn aros mwy na'n tadau,—*
Awn i'r ffordd yr aethant hwythau,
Rhaid yw mynd . . .'

and by the time I've got to the forty-seventh stanza of *The Rubáiyát of Omar Khayyam*,

'When you and I behind the Veil are past,
Oh, but for the long, long while the World shall last,
Which of our Coming and Departure heeds
As the Sea's self should heed a pebble-cast . . .'

I'm crossing the Llanddeusant-Trecastle road already.

I'm getting into the way of walking, and beginning to enjoy it. The dogs have lost something of their early morning exuberance and slog doggedly at my heels through the storm. The wind ruffles their coats, even so near to the ground, and you might suppose they were old before their time.

Beyond the highway is a raised bog, much of it fenced off by the local graziers to prevent their ewes drowning in peaty pools where they seek relief from the flies and heat of summer. As Bob, Jess and myself follow the path that skirts its edge we practically tread on a pair of wild duck, who rise up with heads

9

outstretched and wings flapping. They circle around apparently confused by the unexpected disturbance, or the strange eddies, shapes and shadows of the driven snow. It is comforting to feel that we are not quite alone on the mountain.

A small stream, still running despite the ice, trickles from the end of the bog and becomes stronger and more clearly defined as it flows towards the big dingle of Garreglwyd. Within a fold of the hill a cluster of mountain ponies huddle with their backs to the storm. As we trudge past we can almost feel the damp warmth of their breath, for they don't trouble to move. They have found, as they always find, perhaps the one sheltered spot which gives them best protection from today's particular gale.

There is an ancient track round the steep-sided bank that divides Nant Clydach from Glasfynydd Forest. I've often wondered whether it was just eroded out of the hillside by the passage of feet, horses and carts or whether some lost generation of Welshmen actually set to work with shovels and picks to make the route safe. I would be surprised if the Roman soldiers, camping on Y Pigyn, didn't walk along it as I do now. Whatever its distant origin I am grateful to those who made it, especially today when it doesn't just give me a safe passage across the precipitous mountainside but, nestling below the crest of Fedw Fawr, shelter from the biting wind.

The sky is still heavy and overcast, the clouds purple and the woods beyond dark beneath them. But visibility is ten times better now the swirling snow is no longer blasted into my face by the easterly gale. I make good time on the level, frozen turf towards Rhyblid and the Myddfai mountain.

It is windier and rougher underfoot on the rising ground to the tile vein, a curious outcrop of compressed rock, allegedly running from coast to coast, from the mouth of the river Dee in the far north of the country to the estuary of the Tywi in Carmarthen Bay. People have dug material here for their floors and roofs since building began, but today I'm in no mood for geology. There is another windy ridge to cross before I stand above the Rhyblid mountain fence.

Losing height, and swinging left, I turn from north to south.

I am facing home, and ahead I can see what I'm looking for. A pair of ewes stand, backs to the wind, amongst the tummocky hillocks above the fields of Penrhiw. I hardly need to check the pitch or earmark for I know my sheep by the lie of their wool, the prick of their ears and the turn of their heads. I speak to the dogs and signal for them to run right-handed. They streak across the frozen ground. Their energy has not been dissipated in aimless play, but conserved for this moment, and they go to it with all the skill and enthusiasm of Welsh forwards storming towards the English line.

As I turn up the sheltered path towards Pentregronw our flock of two has increased to twelve, and we pick up a couple more by the turn at the top. They settle down for the long walk home, and it is best not to hustle them along lest one, tired, hungry and perhaps weakened by a wet autumn or grown artful with age, turns off the path and lies down in the rushes or unseen behind an outcrop of rock.

I push them slowly round the Fedw, and count them again and again, for I don't want to leave any behind. I love a hard day on the mountain, but not so much that I want to come round here again tomorrow. We follow the fence from Pentregronw, above Gwydre and Garreglwyd to recross the road by the Llanddeusant grid. As we ford the river Llechau above Blaenllechau we collect another two, and another, and the count has risen to seventeen. It is a longer trip by Aberdyfnant and Llanergoch, but I want to be sure to collect any ewes that may be sheltering beneath Mynydd Llan. We turn left and for a few hundred yards catch the full ferocity of the storm, but the sheep are on their home run, and with two good dogs behind them they are unlikely to double back now.

The daylight has almost gone as they skirt Gellionnen, and it is dark as I turn them into the shelter of Tirbwch. Bob and Jess take their eyes off the sheep as they pass through the mountain gate, for they know at once that then their work is done. They jump up to me for an exuberant expression of mutual congratulation. The first of January, 1997, is over.

Christine Evans

Wednesday 1st January, 1997
Lundy, Fastnet, Irish Sea: N.E. by N. 3-4. Recent snow showers.
Temp: +3 (9a.m.).
Most of England and East Wales is under snow (even two or three inches in the Isle of Man, Heather phoned this morning) but though there were a few flurries of hard white flakes last night, still dry and bright here as it has been since Christmas Eve. The first lambs turned out in Gwagnoe fields have had a good week. Warnings of severe penetrating frost continue, but the sun tempts out walkers and sliding children, and there have been several drownings under ice. While Col. was out last night (fancy dress at the Ship) his friend Rob rang, still a bit high after a narrow escape in the frozen river Leri. He got his dog out but the ice broke under him and he was swept downstream. 'I thought my time had come.' When he scrambled out, the worst thing was the almost paralysing cold. He was six or seven miles from home. Lucky he wasn't, as so often, on his own. He stripped off and took his friend's dry socks, overtrousers and jacket, and they walked back as fast as they could.

I took Peg out for a run through the fields as far as Cwrt pond just after midnight (crystal-brilliant stars, ice gleaming like metal in the ditch, cowpats bleached by frost to sandstone frisbees). Uwchmynydd was ringed with lights—every house lit up, even holiday homes occupied, the giant steel structures of livestock sheds transformed into warm interiors for lambing or last-thing checks on cattle. As I stood and watched, several winked out—Sister Seraphina's in Bronfoel, the visitors in Bryn Sander, all three Brynchwilogs having seen the New Year in. Tonight the whole place is dark, only the orange glow of the light by the telephone kiosk visible under a heavy, overcast sky. A weather change is imminent: Ernest's planning to take the post over to Enlli first thing tomorrow.

Pottered in the garden after breakfast, pale sun surprisingly warm on my back. Pruned the straggliest of the gooseberries—

the old variety Whinham's, I think—once a cutting from Kim's island garden. Long grey tentacles, very spiky, stretching out to the courgette bed and interfering with my runner bean tripod, and though it has very sweet dark red fruit, we have yet to taste more than the odd one—birds always get there first. As the soil softened, I lifted a few potatoes to have with the leg of Enlli lamb for *cinio Dydd Calan*, picked mint from pots in the greenhouse and sprouts (they snapped off easily, brittle with cold.) One wet afternoon soon I must look through the seed catalogues, order at least the early spuds, those small broad beans that stay green, and some shallots; perhaps try out some of the old varieties of tomato from the Soil Association. Getting fingers into the earth and planning what to grow and where is as good a way as any of celebrating the start of a year.

In the afternoon, walk round Anelog, all very still and silent. The *cytiau Gwyddelod*—three hut circles on a rough steep slope to the sea—easy to see under derelict bracken (fox red and crackly) were as alive, perhaps two and a half thousand years old but as current as anything else. The grass where no sun had crept lay limp like grey hair, numb-looking. The well behind Mount stuck out long white tongues of frozen water at the silenced sea. Breath—mine and the dog's—seemed loud, an intrusion.

In the Graveyard

Frost burns the edges
Of wet flowers and the wind
Blows our names away.

Sunday 26th January
S.E. 2 or 3. High pressure over Irish Sea—forecast for week:
calm, little change. Temp: 10.
Strange to see the moon so bold in the morning—like an owl staring in at the kitchen window, throwing bright stripes across the tiles as I fill the kettle for the first *paned* of the day. Calm, uncompromising, not to be relegated to darkness. So much a

presence I get the binoculars to look at its face and turn its bruises into mysterious land-masses and archipelagoes. It travels quite quickly across the window: like a great ship watched out of harbour, so gradually manoeuvred by bow-thrusters and invisible propeller that it feels as if the land has moved. By the time I come back downstairs to drink my tea by the Rayburn, the moon is peeping through the lower conifer branches. By 8 a.m. it's paling, a dried-up seedpod (*lunaria*, of course: the 'moon pennies' Nain and her sisters played with), a ghost apologetically fading.

Sometimes watching feels like being watched: seems to throw consciousness back on itself. A hopelessly egocentric species, we still flirt with a sense of losing ourselves in the infinite; walking the shore watching waves endlessly shaping, endlessly smashing, or lying back on a hillside looking up at fold upon fold of galaxies brings exhilaration—from a sense of limitless possibility? What pain or illness do is reduce the scope so there is no way to pretend each of us is not trapped in a dying body.

As soon as I went outside, Little Owls were calling, and all day as I worked in the garden, one kept coming back to a bramble tangle on the high outside hedge. Rustle and flitter of small birds in every tree—chaffinch and tits making regular trips to the feeder, a goldcrest or two 'sreeing' in the conifers, blackbirds skulking. The top part of the garden is so overgrown perhaps I should let it revert and become a bramble and nettle patch for the birds and butterflies. For the last two Springs, Nain was living with us and I couldn't tackle the rougher work, though she always preferred to be outside, brushing the paths and even the grass.

After lunch, moved young trees—3 whitebeam, several hawthorn, damson, hazel and crabapple—to the new triangular piece enclosed by the high bank of earth left after the road-widening. I plan a wild-flower patch—unmowed until late summer—drifts of bluebells—but first have to establish shelter from the salt gales that are normal here (only half a mile from the sea in three directions) and find a way of eradicating vigorous growths of dock, couch grass, nettle, thistle and creeping buttercup. Old carpet to smother them would be the easiest and most environmentally acceptable, and all it costs is time. Opening up the compost heap discovered a roost of ladybirds tucked up together inside a heap of hollow hogweed stems which I put carefully to one side before barrowing some of the good dark stuff to this year's early spud plot. Poplar suckers have infiltrated the raspberry canes; I think about cutting the tree down, though I love the shiver and wink of its white leaves in early summer.

So all afternoon my hands and brain were busy, planting, planning, noticing swelling buds, and now by the log fire I am pleasantly drowsy. There's more noise in the sea since dark— long, liturgical rhythms, and a moist mist creeping over the fields. Ernest quotes the old saying: *'niwl y gaeaf, gwas yr eira; niwl y gwanwyn, gwas y gwynt'*—fog in winter brings snow; in spring, wind. Nothing else moving, not even any fox cries. Gwilym said he'd shot eleven round Cwrt this winter. Perhaps there aren't any vixens left. I know he has to protect his poultry and pheasants but there is surely a way to leave room for a fox and badger or two.

FEBRUARY

The raven month/*Mis y gigfran*

February is a short sour blackberry of a month, as black as a raven. This is the time of the year when this largest member of the crow family, a croaky-voiced vulture of the sheep country, lays its eggs, even when ice has the land in its grip. The raven times its breeding season to coincide with a period when food is ample—dead sheep on the sheepwalks and carrion galore—its powerful pick-axe of a bill coming in very handy.

Easily identified by its huge bill and diamond- or lozenge-shaped tail, the raven's cry is a croak like that of a heavy duty chain smoker, a deep *kronk* which is the very sound of high crags and unscaleable cliffs. The raven at close quarters reveals itself not to be as black as we proverbially have it, but with feathers which show a sheen of purple and green, black and blue.

Normally shy, ravens have a provenly plentiful intelligence which leads them to sources of ready food and they are familiar scavengers for sandwiches around the summit cafe on Snowdon. There are more pairs of ravens in Wales than in either Scotland or England although the situation today, which is that they are relatively safe from persecution, is a long way removed from, say, a hundred years ago. As many as 120 ravens were killed in Llanfair parish in Meirioneth during 1720-1757 and during the closing years of the last century ravens were killed in great numbers. A total of 464 ravens were killed during the 28 years ending in 1902 on Lord Penrhyn's estate, which embraced some of the highlands of Snowdonia.

Wales now has one of the largest roosts of ravens in the world, with up to two thousand winging their way to the sitka spruce sanctuary of Newborough Warren in the south-west corner of the isle of Anglesey.

Cigfrain yn hedeg yn uchel, ravens flying high, was held as a sign of high winds in the Welsh countryside and the bird makes its presence known in place names such as Tap y Gigfran or Craig Nyth y Gigfran. It has always had a relationship with man, and raven remains have been found in a Port Eynon cave on the Gower coast in south Wales which date back to the early

Holocene period, somewhere between 9,000 and 6,000 years ago, while elsewhere in Britain remains have been found which show that the bird was flying around in the perishing cold of the Pleistocene age. The raven itself can live a long time—one in Stockholm lived to the ripe old age of eighty!

It is a bird which makes an appearance in legends and literature galore, in far corners of the world, from Noah's ark-raven to the one Charles Dickens gave Barnaby Rudge. The war god and king of the gods in Norse mythology, Odin, had two ravens, Hugin and Munin, Thought and Memory, who were dispatched to fly each day around the world gathering information, returning of an evening to perch on the king's shoulders and report on what they'd seen.

The roving Norseman Floki Vilgerdsson set out in AD 846 on a voyage of discovery taking ravens with him which he set loose in mid ocean. The birds flew high to spy out the nearest land, and Vilgerdsson followed in the direction they eventually took. His bird guides took him to an island which he then called Iceland.

The bird features frequently in Shakespeare, coming 'oe'er my memory/as doth the raven o'er the infectious house/ Boding to all' in *Othello*.

As an omen of imminent slaughter the raven would have been an unwelcome sight. A man who wrote most lyrically about ravens in Wales, George Bolam, writing about one of the raven's other names, noted the fact that 'The expression "Corby messenger" had a more sinister meaning, associated with coming strife and bloodshed, with its attendant glut of carrion; and in the days of Hywel Dda or Owain Glyndŵr, the ravens of the Dee valley must have chanted their hoarse requiem over many a stricken field, of which they had, perhaps, been looked upon as the forerunners.'

Even away from battlefields, if chance arises it seems that this bird will feast on human flesh—a murder in rural Wales was reported on the basis of a pair of ravens croaking over the corpse. Such stories contribute much to the creature's black and sinister reputation.

Nevertheless, during the winter I often reroute my journeys north through Wales to watch the ravens gathering at the Tylwch tip near Llanidloes. Wheeling against a white sky ominous with snow the ravens are survivors of harsh times and difficult places. Birds of ill omen, they are also spirits of wild Wales, their calls almost sub-sonically breaking up the stillness of a wanly-lit afternoon.

William Condry

February 15

We hear today that by a remarkably fine piece of seamanship a large, fully laden oil tanker called *Sea Empress* has been driven in perfectly fine weather on to rocks at the approaches to Milford Haven. It is an accident that conservationists have feared might afflict that wildlife-rich coast ever since Milford became an oil port 36 years ago.

February 25

We have watched with increasing horror as the grounding of the *Sea Empress* has led to the spilling of maybe 80,000 tons of oil into the sea, all due, it is being said, to the incompetence of those in charge since the accident. What is certain is that large number of scoters, guillemots and razorbills have already come ashore alive or dead, leaving us to wonder how many others have been lost at sea. Shellfish and marine plants must also have suffered severely along the many miles of shoreline now known to be affected by oil.

February 27

If challenged I would have to admit that, apart from frequently trespassing on it in pursuit of plants, birds and butterflies, I do not use the railway as much as I should. But I did go by train to the Midlands today, and much enjoyed the relief from the ever increasing strain of car-driving. Here we have a miraculously surviving railway that leaves the Dyfi valley near Machynlleth, struggles bravely uphill mile after mile to reach the watershed, then drops gently down to the valley of the Severn (or Hafren). It was close to the Severn that my train stopped briefly at the village of Caersws. No one got off or on, but no matter; Caersws may be a very small place but if you have even the slightest feeling for history you would do well to alight there. For in stepping on to its platform you would be stepping on to the embankment of a Roman fort. It says much about official nineteenth-century vandalism that a slice was quite cheerfully taken off the corner of a Roman fort to build this line. Today we expect better treatment for our ancient monuments.

I like the Roman period. Though far back in time, it is more easily grasped than the centuries that followed, those well-named Dark Ages so rife with make-believe and legends, so thin in real history. Not that for one moment I am suggesting I would have liked the Romans themselves. I don't doubt they were every bit as arrogant, bloodthirsty and cruel as all other master nations, past, present or future.

You can have fun at Caersws trying to trace the roads the Romans made north, south, east and west. The most intriguing to me has always been the road that must have gone west over the hills to the forts not far from the Ceredigion coast at Capel Bangor and Trawsgoed. But yesterday, on the train, I was eastward bound for England and it was not until I reached Shrewsbury, which had a Roman city at nearly Wroxeter, that I realised, looking at a map, that I had come from Caersws by way of another Roman fort at Forden, the Severn being the link all the way. So the train follows pretty closely the trail blazed by the Romans, or someone before them.

The fourth of February is a significant date in the life of a sheep farmer, for it marks the beginning of the hundred-day retention period for Hill Livestock Compensatory Allowances and the Sheep Annual Premium Scheme. From now until midnight on the fifteenth of May we must keep the number of sheep declared on form SAP/HLCA 2 (1997) and be able to say at any time just where they are, and produce them for inspection and counting without notice. We cannot sell them or move them from one farm to another without telling the Welsh Office beforehand.

I suppose to the ordinary tax-payer, Brussels civil servant or Welsh Office official it seems quite reasonable. If very large sums of public money are being used to support the farming community it shouldn't be dished out recklessly. If claims went unchecked, subsidies could be paid on phantom sheep and the whole policy brought into disrepute. But does anyone in Cardiff or Carmarthen have any idea how it feels to know that any time, whatever else was planned for the day, you might have to gather the flock? Outlying ewes could be heaven knows where, from Llyn y Fan Fawr to Mynydd Bach, with some perhaps strayed over the top into the distant coal country of the Swansea valley, seven miles over the peaks and over twenty by the road. It is a time of unbelievable tension and nervous stress, for the financial penalties of failure to comply are out of all proportion to the magnitude of the offence, and the fear of being labelled in some official file as dishonest too dreadful to live with.

And it is unnecessary. In former times the farmer and the field officer, the official who actually counts the sheep, would arrange a mutually convenient date in advance. The visit would be expected, and the flock would be gathered ready in the fields. To borrow sheep off a neighbour was impossible, for every flock has its individual earmark recorded in a book and attempts to tamper with them would be obvious. One thing is certain, whoever framed the regulations never shepherded on an unenclosed mountain in winter.

So in February I took three days off to go for a walk from Tregaron to Haverfordwest, and three more to go for a longer walk through Pembroke, Tenby, Carmarthen, Neath and Maesteg to the Rhondda valley. What an escape! What a variety of lives in so small a compass!

Back at the farm I hired a bit of help to keep an eye on the place. While I was off enjoying my walk he was renewing the loft floor, a worm-infested bats' paradise that has been a safety hazard for forty years. He was, need I say, instructed to disclaim any knowledge whatsoever of the whereabouts of me or my sheep to any callers wearing a tie or carrying a file and clip-board.

Because of the way the regulations are, February and March has become a good time for selling breeding sheep. I have a small bunch wintering on rented ground a few miles north of Carmarthen and another just inland from Cardigan Bay. Prices were tremendous in Llanybydder mart at the beginning of the month, so on the seventeenth I took a trailer load from Pantricket. The Cardis must have known I was coming, for the trade was well down. Two weeks later I took a lot from Blaenffos. Never mind west Wales, next winter I'll be off to the West Indies if I get a few more days like that!

Llanybydder is the place for selling sheep, but it is Abergavenny for buying hay. When I began my working life self-sufficiency was the target of every self-respecting farmer. To buy hay was to admit a measure of failure, to sell it suggested the bank was breathing down your neck. To do either was considered a poor business. I set out with good intentions, making hay off tiny meadows with worn machines, and none wore more than the muscles of my back. Grazing cattle in summer and spending the margin on purchased fodder from flatter fields than mine, made with more expensive equipment than my acreage could justify, proved a far better bet.

At first I bought from merchants who made more out of every load than I did. Then I bought by the barnful in Herefordshire, selling the surplus to pay for the transport and sometimes

24

doing so well I had my own requirements for next to nothing. But now that I am old, and have paid off the mortgage, I just go over to Abergavenny to buy a load as I need it. The lorries are lined up round the back of the cattle pens and are sold by auction at half past one. Buying hay is an art, for it is a product of infinite variety. It changes in quality not just from field to field but within a field, depending on the day it was cut and the time it was carried. It is an art which necessity has forced me to master.

But between filling in forms on the kitchen table, days at the mart and days on the road, fixing the loft floor and selling the sheep, the quickly forgotten incidents of a farming life, there is one event in February 1997 I will not forget. On Tuesday the eighteenth the old dog Wimpole was so worn and failing he could no longer keep on his feet. Zenecarp and woolly blankets could do nothing more for him and I buried him beyond the apple trees after eighteen years together.

A stock farmer cannot afford the indulgence of sentimental affection towards his animals, but there are some that stick in the memory in spite of ourselves. A few dogs, the black cow Hairy Mary I milked every morning for sixteen years with only the briefest interval between one calf and the next, a couple of horses—and they not the best. But Wimpole was something special. I remember him sorting my sheep from strays on the bald top of Fan Foel while I stood across the dingle of Nant Melyn on Cefn Esgyrn, the hill of bones, or when he swam in the Usk with my son Jason, then in primary school, or him lying by the door when I came downstairs, pretending to know nothing about the warm hollow among the cushions of my most comfortable chair.

'For some we loved, the loveliest and the best
    That from his Vintage rolling Time hath prest,
Have drunk their Cup a Round or two before,
    And one by one crept silently to rest.'

Rest in peace, old friend.

Christine Evans

Saturday February 1st
S/S.E. 4-5. Sleet at times.
'If Candlemas dawn bright and clear, there'll be two winters in the year': so perhaps we should welcome the overcast sky and wet snow slipping off the trees. Used the last of the Bramleys stored in the old caravan to make apple and cherry cake. Snowdrops making a brave show. One of my favourites—the clumps of leaves making patches of colour under shrubs when little else is growing, and then the drifts of flowers with their gentle fragrance and the bright green pattern inside, delicate as painted china, leading down towards yellow stamens. Dwarf iris in pots in the greenhouse are in flower—blue and purple—and the kitchen is scented by three lovely white hyacinths (Rita's Christmas present, carefully labelled *L'Innocence*.) It's only just occurred to me that early spring flowers are almost invariably scented or strongly marked; to attract the few insects there are around, though having bulbs, they don't need to set seed.

Thursday 6th February
S W. gale 8 to severe gale 9. Intermittent slight rain. Temp: 6/7.
Ernest to Lighthouse by helicopter from RAF Valley base—took 40 minutes to get there against the wind but only 10 minutes back!

Home late after Parents' Evening at college, noticed daffodils by torchlight—an inch or two above ground, strong thrusting points aiming at light as purposeful as rockets from Cape Canaveral. Humid and drizzly by now: 'growing weather'. Enid's geraniums that I'm 'sitting' while she's wintering in Spain are in full, bright red flower on the landing windowsill. I must remember to put the early potatoes to chit in the loft above the garage where there's plenty of light but not too much heat, to encourage strong shoots.

Reading 'Promised Lands' by Jane Gardam—the First Fleet's landing in Australia—but it didn't succeed in switching my

26

mind off tonight—when I did get to sleep my dreams of mossy steps in a walled garden (Plas Tan-y-Bwlch perhaps?) were troubled by images of destruction and vandalism. Downstairs for a hot milk drink at 3.30, scribbling: Nain died two months ago tonight.

ANNIVERSARIES

'This time yesterday'—
Last Friday, a week ago,
Sixth day of each month.

Six months: her birthday.
A first hayfield without her.
Another Christmas.

Slowly the earth turns,
Pulls winter over her face
Slowly the grave heals.

Sunday 9th February
S.W.5 to 6 Visibility good.
'There was a roaring in the wind all night'—a strong south-westerly which has cleared the sky. (Esther's talk of 'doing' Wordsworth for A Level coursework perhaps put the line into my head.) Straight out into the garden: raked the best-drained garden plot and put in the garlic sent up from Lampeter by Jenny. The sun warm but very pale—yolk of a supermarket egg, or a clouded glass marble. Chaffinches and blackbirds in fine song in the trees.

Mid-morning, walked down to Aberdaron to get the Sunday paper. A good walk, this: twenty minutes of fields and green lane, about the same of windy cliff-top, gorse scrub in bloom, then across the river and along the shore. The cliff path was squelchy after two nights of drizzle, with pools of standing water. 'Plashy': (*Resolution and Independence* again) and though there was no sign of the hare scattering rainbows the dog did her best (hopeless to keep a Labrador dry on a walk in *any* season). The sea was aggressively shiny, roaring right up to the base of the cliff and a heavy swell breaking white on the Gwylan Islands in the bay. I stopped by the ruined cottage—Penrallt—that's slowly being swallowed by ivy , and poked about a bit for any sign of a well. In summer adders nest here—last year I surprised three young ones basking by the front door. Its windows look out over nothing but sea; like being on the deck of a ship a hundred feet above the waterline. There were oystercatchers exchanging pairing notes too low down for me to see, and a raven creaked overhead. I stood in bright sunlight but the far end of the beach tailed off into mist; Rhiw didn't exist.

Big tides so wide stretches of shining sand invited running, skimming along dizzily among blown foam like scudding cumulus, air and earth and water all mixed up and flowing. Waveprints dissolved into silver froth as I stood and watched and the sea's roaring and thudding drowned all thought except the pleasure of being able to walk for an hour without seeing anyone. In winter, there's not even any aircraft noise—only, occasionally, sunlight glints on the slipstream of a high trajectory jet making for Shannon or arcing across the Atlantic at 30,000 feet.

Monday 10th February
S.W. gale force 8, veering N.W. 8 to severe gale 9,
occasionally storm 10. Hail showers.
Dark and stormy all day. High water about 6 a.m., so Ernest went down to Porth to move the boat higher up the beach. Lot · of students absent from college—the combination of big tides and wind-driven sea caused flooding at Barmouth and Afonwen so the trains couldn't run into Pwllheli (the road was closed at Riverside as well so traffic from this end was diverted.) Violent hail clattering on the roof drowned my teaching in the lecture room. I drove down to the seafront at lunchtime—big waves gulping oxygen, a deep throbbing from the rocks.

The light was odd, eclipse-like, as I drove home about 5 o' clock. From Mynytho hill a sun pale as the moon stood over Rhiw mountain—so drained and anaemic it was almost naked-looking, in shock. By the time I came over Rhoshirwaun, there was a sliver of new moon high up in the south-west and it was getting dark rapidly, the wind already shifted to the north.

A black and destructive night. Ernest was out at a Fisherman's Meeting in Nefyn, and I huddled in front of a smoky log fire, recording snippets of radio plays and sound effects for a scriptwriting class, watching the curtains quiver and wondering how long the electricity cables could stand up to the mauling. At eleven, the rain stopped and I took the dog out in the back field. The stars were all muffled against the cold and there was no sign of the moon. The foghorn from the island reached me in gusts of wet air.

Ernest brought news of a tree down across the road in Nanhoron.

In the night the wind dropped so suddenly it woke me. It was 4.15. I imagined huddled lambs too lifting their heads. How do the small birds survive?

Saturday 16th February
Intense Atlantic low approaching. N.W. 4, veering S.E. 5-6,
increasing 7 to gale 8 later. Squally showers of sleet or snow later.
Clear and bright, surprisingly calm. Ernest and Col. (home after exams) crossed to Enlli with post, sheep nuts, goatfood, dogfood, a sack of flour and Tim's boar semen that's been in the fridge since Next Day Delivery on Wednesday—prompting many jokes about whose tea it should be used in, etc. Hope the sow is still in season; pigs are tricky and the rare breed semen (Oxford Sandy and Black) doesn't come cheap.

I sent over a few supplies and a huge bar of Cadbury's chocolate for Dot with a note saying it was four months' supply—to last her till the baby's born.

Washed a thick rime of salt off the windows, only realising how little could be seen when the sun came out. Steely sunlight, a morning of glitter and splinters, tinfoil flashes from the waxy evergreen leaves of the euonymus bushes and even the tips of moss on the wall. Spring light is especially harsh, paring away what's old and rotten.

Monday 24th February
N.W. 6-7 Blustery showers followed by continuous moderate rain.
The t.v. weather map shows a series of deep depressions are rolling over us like ripples in a pond. There's been a week of storm and floods. Off work for the second time—fluey, headache, now a chest infection that makes me feel not-quite-real, so in bed half-reading, half-remembering the winter of 1947—a stern voice on the radio warning of icebergs in the Channel and the need to save fuel.

MARCH

Gannets/*Huganod*

In those wonderful tales *The Mabinogion* there is a tree which burns bright with green leaves on one side while the other half is all aflame. This sort of poetic division can be plainly seen by passengers of the ferries that ply back and fore between Wales and Ireland. They pass the island of Grassholm, eight miles off the Pembrokeshire coast—which at a distance seems to be half black and half white. Up close, the white resolves itself into tens of thousands of gannets, bright white birds with six-foot wing spans ending in black tips—which only serve to underline the white brightness of their cigar-shaped bodies.

Birds arrive in March to open the summer feeding and breeding season on this tiny island. April sees major league activity. Gannets build messy nests, between one and two feet high, made up of anything and everything they find in the sea. Unfortunately this sort of magpie-like collecting of floating nesting material includes discarded fishing line and the young gannets often find themselves inextricably tangled in lengths of the stuff which binds them agonisingly to their own nests.

One autumn I went on a mission to rescue such trapped young birds on an island which turns out to have more connections with the Mabinogion. Its old name is Gwales, the magic island beyond time where seven men returning from a campaign in Ireland rested awhile, well, eighty years in total, with only the head of Bendigeidfran, or Brân, the 'crowned king of the Isle of Britain' to keep them company. They did not age and a sort of blissful amnesia froze out all thought of former sorrows, that is until an inquisitive Heilyn fab Gwyn opened the door which faces Aber Henfelen and Cornwall. But lest anyone think that this gateway to Annwfn or the Otherworld is a mere literary figment I should perhaps tell you that in the sky above us as we walked the island looking for trapped gannets was a flock of birds. A mixed flock of birds, it contained two species: swallows, the birds of summer—ready to depart for Africa, and redwings, birds of winter, newly arrived from Russia or Scandinavia. That day the island was truly the crossroads of the seasons, though we found no door. Sadly we found plenty of gannets. In extreme cases we had to amputate legs if the twine had eaten too deeply into the leg as the bird twisted and struggled to get free.

Gannets are gregarious nesters, the birds spaced out across the island which is the second largest gannetry in the whole wide world. They have been spreading year by year, with a population which has gone from the hundreds of pairs of the early decades of the century to the tens of thousands of today. At the peak of the nesting season the spectacle can easily rival that of African big game. There is a great cacophony, a football crowd frenzy which grows as incomers coast in at evening.

Gannet heads are yellow and the eyes are a piercing blue, the colour of tropical seas. Young birds will have seen such seas on their journey from their wintering grounds off the coasts of North and West Africa. The adult birds move out into the North Atlantic when they leave the island in September and October.

It is as a fisherman that the gannet truly excels. The white colour of gannets is ideal for a bird which fishes by diving down from the sky. Its favourite food in the breeding season is herring and mackerel. The latter swim in deep water and only the gannet is able to plunge down far enough to feed on this nutritious species. The birds may fly as far as three hundred miles from the colony to feed. From a height of some thirty feet the wings close and crumple and the dagger-like bill becomes a living spear-head. The bird's design cushions the blow as the bird hits water from a height, for the skulls are strengthened and a system of air-sacs also help absorb the shock of impact. Lucky observers will be able to see the bird's underwater wake, a green fizz of sherbet as it tunnels through and churns up water. Most fish aren't speared, in fact: they are simply gobbled up as the bird plunges through the water. Other gannets, spotting such success, are attracted to the scene and soon the area is alive with feeding birds.

At times like these it is easy to see why human greed and hunger are often compared to those of the gannet, that plunging fisherman dropping from sky to sea.

L aid low by a bad dose of 'flu, I was unable to get out at night to hear the delicious concert of *nachtmusic* that comes each March with the movement of curlews to the hills. But I enjoyed it at second hand when a friend phoned me after dark on the 17th to report that his farmer-neighbour had just phoned him to say that many curlews were passing overhead up the Dyfi valley, filling the night with their liquid cries. He marvelled that they should move up in this weather when the moorlands where they will nest are still deep in snow. This March return of the curlews is a signal of spring the upland shepherds look forward to: it is their equivalent of lowlanders hearing the first chiffchaff in the woods. I felt happy to think that farmers phone each other about curlews as well as about market prices. Curlew time is also Bewick's swan time. These elegant fowl winter in Ireland and fly over this part of Cardigan Bay every March to their continental breeding grounds. It is quite magical to see them, perhaps a dozen or twenty or more, passing high overhead, gleaming white in the sunshine, dropping their gentle music earthwards as they go steadily on along their eastward flight line over the Cambrian Mountains.

One night I went badger-watching. Have you ever tried to walk quietly through an oakwood at night? And cursed the dead leaves crackling under every step? But once you have sat down by a badger's sett, those leaves become your ally. They tell you about the movements of whatever creatures may be stirring on the floor of the wood. In the absolute silence of a windstill night, deep in the heart of a wood, even three-inch animals like bank voles and wood mice are remarkably noisy as they scurry among the leaves. A hedgehog rummaging about is something you can hear a hundred yards away. A fox trotting by, no matter how delicately, sounds as if he is bursting through like an elephant. But the real rowdies are the badgers. They may have little to say but they make up for it by crashing about among the leaves as if for the fun of it. Their nest-making can be noisy too—they gather armfuls of leaves and drag them backwards into the sett, and you can imagine what a row that makes.

* * *

Bird of the month, despite the lovely Bewick's swans, was the Cetti's warbler I heard as soon as I reached the far-spreading reed-beds at the mouth of the Teifi River that separates Ceredigion from Pembrokeshire. These marshes, now a West Wales Wildlife Trust reserve, are a fine slice of wilderness and a worthy breeding place for this warbler that has accomplished such an astonishing northward spread across Europe and first reached the Teifi in the mid-nineties. Even if you don't manage to see the bird its song is an instant give-away—a brief explosion of loud, spluttering notes unlike the utterance of any other bird. On my visit at the end of March I not only heard three in song but, from a hide, I actually got a good view of one as it perched briefly on the topmost twig of a bush. It was, in bright sunlight, quite a rich red-brown on head and back, pale-grey underneath. I was lucky, for Cetti's is one of those warblers that delight in playing hide and seek with birdwatchers.

Also late in the month I walked up one of our local valleys to clear the final vestiges of 'flu from my lungs. I went to check on two evergreen ferns that grow in the thunder and spray of a waterfall. I was curious to see how well they had wintered. One of them, the Tunbridge filmy-fern, is tiny, its fronds only an inch or two long, and it would hardly ever be noticed if it did not form quite large mats on the faces of wet rocks and tree trunks. I found the hanging curtains of this little fern in excellent condition: evidently it had laughed its way through all the weeks of frost. My other waterfall fern—the hay-scented buckler fern—stood about two and a half feet high. It had not come through the winter untouched by Jack Frost but it still stood upright and was in better shape than the nearby fronds of the common buckler-fern lying flat on the ground in complete despair. I came home relieved that our parish's two rarest ferns had each got through March better than I had.

M arch already, and there's still a lot to do before the place is ready for the lambing season. But first Salisbury Plain, to check the ewe hoggs, the yearlings, wintering on a dairy and arable farm where there's scarcely a field into which my whole place couldn't fit without a squeeze. Ever since I learnt to count I've asked myself why the poorest and roughest farms are so small, and the most fertile so vast. I think they call it capitalism. The new Severn crossing may be a masterpiece of engineering, but getting to and fro along the M4 is a nightmare. Very few can pilot an aeroplane or drive a train, but almost everyone thinks they can manage a motorcar. The next generation will really have to do something about this.

Once past Beaufortshire, with its wire-netting guards to keep hounds off the motorway, I turn south, skirting Chippenham and through the lovely stone town of Devizes. A bit of well-wooded up-and-down country and I'm into the rolling expanse of the great plain. Two things strike me most—it's not flat, and the power of the military occupation is all-pervasive. My sheep, grazing a tank range, are fat as pigs and enjoying it.

With a couple of hours to spare before racing home I choose between Stonehenge and Salisbury cathedral. Stonehenge wins on the basis of seniority, but I'm not allowed amongst the stones. In fact you have to pay to cross the road from the car park. Not so much a monument as a marketing opportunity.

> 'They say the Lion and the Lizard keep
> The Courts where Jamshyd gloried and drank deep:
> And Bahrám, that great Hunter —-the Wild Ass
> Stamps o'er his Head, but cannot break his Sleep.'

Better that than £3.70 a head with complimentary headphones and audio cassette.

Next morning I'm putting up lambing shelters. Three sections of half-round corrugated tin held down with a tight wire, secured to a couple of well driven stakes. The weather I fear at this or any season isn't rain or hail or snow, drought or flood, but wind. One of the first things a baby sheep learns is how and where to escape from it.

The lean-to shed over the road has to be cleaned clean-clean. I will use it to shelter orphan lambs, problem ewes short of milk or on a course of antibiotics and ewes who have lost their own offspring and are having an unwelcome substitute forced upon them. I like this shed. Forty-five feet by twenty, oak stanchions, rafters 8' x 3', a dwarf wall of blocks and a tidy floor of 6" concrete that I hand mixed and laid in a single day. I built it over a quarter of a century ago, and last year Jared Lane re-roofed it with full length coated sheets, dark green, with sky lights, fluorescent tubes and tidy tongue and groove cladding on the pine ends. Every year I try to do one or two major works. A new roof, painting and decorating my house inside and out, building a nice range of kennels, planting a few thousand trees, putting in a new septic tank or putting up some fancy gates to deter unwelcome visitors. Whatever need is most pressing and however far the money will go. The big job at the moment is the loft floor.

The first lambs are due on the twenty-fifth of March, and on the fourteenth I begin the serious business of vaccinating the ewes to protect the newborn from seven clostridial diseases. The two that really concern me are tetanus, from which I've lost two ponies and an uncertain number of sheep, and lamb dysentery, which would wipe out a high proportion of the crop if it had the chance. I didn't vaccinate in 1961, and as the losses escalated from the unacceptable to the catastrophic I was running round the field trying to catch the little lambs before they hit the ground to give them the inoculation which alone could save them. From that year to this I have never again chanced my luck, but given protection in advance with a double injection to immunise the flock.

Before I begin the flock must be gathered, but with longer days and soft, damp weather and the odd few hours of sunshine, that is a far easier task than it was in January. My two old horses, Firs and Frazzle, are shod and pressed into service. The gelding Firs, by a Cleveland Bay out of a black pony mare taking a year and a half off to recover from a fractured elbow, herself by a thoroughbred from a Welsh cob cross Arab mare that I bought from the Urdd camp at Llangrannog not years but decades ago, is a ponderous but obliging fellow who has never put me down or let me down in his life. Frazzle the mare is a complete contrast. Always in a hurry, her grandfather is Firs's father. Her mother was conceived on the same day as Firs, by a really big, old fashioned thoroughbred well into her thirties the day she produced her mother, and finally taken to Bristol at the age, I think, of thirty-seven. Frazzles's father was Cefngoernoeth's Welsh cob from Llangadog, and she herself is on the go from dawn to dusk, apparently never tires and is so active and supple she never tires you out either. However, she has tripped and fallen a couple of times on the mountain—just absent-minded, I think.

Between the two of them and the dogs most of the flock are gathered first go, and the furthest stragglers brought in over the following week. Injecting is a slow business, for the ewes are heavy in lamb and must be handled as gently as possible. You can buy automatic syringes that pump the vaccine out of the bottle as you jab one sheep then another, but I prefer the less brutal technique of drawing out each dose individually by hand. Conveyor belt medicine is not for me or my animals. A good friend over Bethlehem way once boasted to me how many sheep he could treat in a morning, and three weeks later he was complaining at how often the vaccines didn't work. I don't know if he learnt from his experience, but I certainly did.

The first lamb arrived on the fifteenth of March. Ten days later the count had risen to thirty, and the season proper began. The ewe hoggs came home in a hired lorry on the twenty-sixth, and the following day were dosed, marked and injected and sent on to the mountain. By the end of the month no ewe had died, and the lamb losses were under five percent. The bitch Nell had puppies, but only three, so the sheep, biologically speaking, were doing a good bit better than the dogs!

Monday 3rd March
N. 3 becoming variable Poor visibility at times.
'The first mild day of March'—woke to birdsong, warm sun, calm air. Col. (home to complete the water survey for his dissertation) went with Ernest to take the post over to Enlli—first time in 16 days a crossing's been possible. The Trust's first crossing of the year too so the new Island Manager and his wife could have a look; they are to go and stay later in the month. He's already announcing that they'll be living on Enlli till he retires—usually a bad sign.

As I drove to work, could see Steve Ship's boat crossing Aberdaron Bay—carrying first of the season's lobster pots out. That will get the other fishermen going.

Drizzly fog came down about 3. I got home to foghorn sounding clearly from Enlli. Walked on the headland through a sort of grey muslin. Half an hour was enough.

At half-past midnight, startled out of sleep by the telephone —Trinity House in Harwich, where all lighthouses are controlled now, had lost contact with Bardsey Lighthouse—would Ernest report that the light was o.k. and cross as early as possible to carry out a full check.

Wednesday 5th March
N. 5 backing S.6 to gale 8.
Finished in college early so went to Cae Llo Brith in Llanystumdwy to thank Sali for looking after me on Saturday at Coleg Harlech. By the Dwyfor the snowdrops that were so magnificent—great drifts of them—are over, superceded by the sharper green daffodil leaves and first buds. Moss on the tree trunks seemed to reflect sunlight—almost unnaturally bright.

Tired this evening. 'Mae'r gwanwyn yn gryf,' says Iona, our neighbour up the hill; 'spring drains all the energy out of you.' I flick through last Sunday's *Times*, becoming absorbed in comment on 'The Killing of the Countryside' by Graham Harvey (the reviewers unite in snootiness about his being agricultural story editor of The Archers, but it does mean he knows about policies and pollutants.) I begin reading with sympathy—I too hate the idea of the country as a food factory—but feel an excess of righteous indignation in the indictment of 'farmers who have comprehensively wrecked and near lost us our land.' I know I'm lucky to live in an area which hasn't gone over to intensive monoculture; perhaps I haven't seen the whole picture, but I've lived among farming people most of my life and while some may be greedy and a few even cruel, they can't be more to blame than the policy-makers (often investors), the businessmen and the consumers who demand ever-cheaper food. How can Kwiksave sell eggs at 29p a half-dozen and Leo's a large roasting chicken for 3.99? When we buy them we are condoning things like the use of growth-promoters, the feeding of ground-up waste; closing our minds to how the animals pay. I wish subsidies should be re-directed to sustainable small-scale, nature-friendly farming—so no-one draws grants of up to £100,000.

The picture chosen to illustrate the article *Destroying the Fields of Our Dreams?* is of a spot above Llangollen; it shows heather moorland and a green valley, patchworked into irregular hedged fields with trees; there's a bit of ploughland and browner hill pasture. It doesn't show the 54-seater coaches, caravans and holidaymakers' cars nose-to-tailing it into Wales: the land as rural theme park doesn't appeal to me either.

Sunday 9th March
N. to N.W. 3-4.
The year's biggest tide so far. Aberdaron beach at low water was a wide vast stretch of dry, ribbed sand. The black timbers of the old jetty at Porth Samdde like a double row of ancient vertebrae; closer, each was festooned with ribbons and tangles of weed where small green crabs and sealice scuttled. One or two good lumps of timber had been washed in, and a palette of useful size that I dragged up to the mouth of the stream before walking over to Porth Meudwy to meet Ernest and Col. who were due back about 4 from their monthly 'Attendant's Duties'

at the lighthouse. Primroses and dog-violets beside the cliff path. The cove was a different place with all its rocks exposed—great slabs like toffee at the soft-set stage, smooth grey seal or dolphin shapes as well as harder cubes and sills ridged and scratched by the glacier that tumbled all together and carved out the valley. Graptolites, fossil worms from the Silurian period—the time of the first vertebrates and land plants, 440 million years ago—can be found here. On the east side towards the village the rock is almost plum colour—the vein of jasper that was quarried in Uwchmynydd a hundred years ago for Victorian ladies' washstands.

Andrew, the Bardsey Warden, was on the beach waiting to go back to the island so I had up-to-date news of Sarah and the children—she has been adapting one of the barns as a schoolroom.

Later: there's been a lot in the papers about this comet with the funny name—Hale-Bopp—but what a surprise to see it pointing down at Tegfan, the little house at the top of our back field, exactly like an arrow piercing the earth as Tolstoy described Halley's. Without binoculars it's like a spill of luminous paint across the sky. Focussed in, you can see the great round core and its brilliant tail like a giant sperm. It is a startling presence in the clear night sky; ironic that we welcome it, go out to feast our eyes on its bright 'hair' (ancient Greek *kome* = hair) when to our ancestors it would have been an omen of 'dis-aster'. Before bed, I search my school-prize copy of *War and Peace* for the moment when, unaware of the impending battle of Borodino and the burning of Moscow, Pierre Bezuhov exults in the 'white light and long uplifted tail (of) the brilliant comet of the year 1812, which was said to portend all sorts of horrors and the end of the world. With rapture and his eyes wet with tears he contemplated the radiant star which, after travelling in its orbit with inconceivable velocity through infinite space seemed suddenly to remain fast in one chosen spot in the black firmament . . .'

Tuesday 11th March
S.W. 3-4.

To lunch with Geoff in Waunfawr. Sunny and warm as summer—drove with both windows down through wafts of birdsong and gorse in brilliant bloom all along the hedges. We sat among daffodils, crocus and hellebores in the garden with cats Mali and Melyn, eat leek soup, home-made bread, goat's cheese, olives and sundried tomatoes, and talk about the village in Crete where Geoff takes a yoga course each May.

Not working on Tuesdays makes a real difference, but I've decided to give in my notice and give up teaching this summer. Especially now the new block has shut off my view of the trees and the sea . . . There are too many things I want to do. After supper (not dark now till after 6) I potted seedlings, planted 4 rows of potatoes (second earlies—the *Sharpe's Express* are already well up), sowed parsnips, lettuce and beetroot before going up to Brynawelon where Viv's having a few days' holiday. Once Observatory Warden on an island only 2 miles long, she has 2000 miles of waterway habitat from Inverness to Gloucestershire to look after now.

Sunday 16th March

Ravens very vocal this morning—makes us suspicious of a dead sheep nearby.

With Kim and Gwydion, drove over to Plas Gelliwig for a load of logs (two buzzards dancing in the sky above Sarn Meillteyrn). Gwydion's family home, for sale; once the centre of an estate, a whole community with its own chapel and waterwheel—17 acres of mixed woodland, overgrown and insecty on the paths to the lake—formal gardens, sunken lawn, big old trees, layers of leafmould smothering gravel walks; walled kitchen garden with box hedges and pergola for vines, orchard with mulberry tree, glasshouse with heating pipes still intact, dovecot . . . Inside, the house has something of the grandeur of Gregynog. A long row of brass bells, still named, in the kitchen. I liked the atmosphere in the spacious cellars; much vigorous servant life had gone on down there. Sad to see the decay of such a place; instead of creating 'new manor houses' for the millennium as Gummer announced this week, perhaps there should be support for restorations where a number of people could live in self-contained apartments, enough to maintain house and grounds.

The first primroses are out in the hedges—fewer each year. By Minafon—a mile from the village—a middle-aged couple were shamelessly carrying trowel and half-full plastic bag. Decent-looking people, just greedy or thoughtless.

Friday 21st March Equinox
Picking last of purple sprouting broccoli—3 months; leeks, curly kale, cabbages.

Two woodpigeons back to nest in hawthorns behind garage —mind-numbing crooning from 5.30 a.m., then three of them flying round with high-pitched girly shrieks—*Oooh! Aaah!*—and picking at precious spring greens.

Cloudy all this week—no comet till tonight. At 5 a.m. it's high in the sky above Anelog, tail streaming westwards now. Impossible to realise the speed at which it's moving—62,000 miles an hour.

Saturday 22th March
Easter holidays. Had planned for Enlli but sea grey and sulky with spiteful heaves and a rising swell. After lifting his pots on the north coast, Steve got into some difficulty coming back round Braich-y-Pwll and eventually had to run before the sea all the way up to Nefyn. His trainee crewman lectured sternly about a father's responsibility, and when they got into shelter, Steve noticed he'd inflated his life-jacket and tied buoys to each leg. If he'd gone into the water he'd have been in some trouble—upside down!

Sunday 23rd March (Palm Sunday)
Traditionally, 'flower Sunday'—when families go together to decorate graves. Very cold and miserable. Blackthorn in full blossom (sign of a cold spell). A deadness to its white, like thin

44

froth or rice; a grudging quality, as though it absorbs light, though individually each flower is a tiny star.

Friday 28th March
Drizzle, rain. Mist, chilly. Driving to work, noticed the first hawthorn leaves bright green like dashes of new paint on dark-metal, and the plum tree in the garden's in flower.
Easter holidays begin. All day sorting out coursework files.

Sunday 30th March
Enlli—taking Gwydion who has a week's repair work at Cristin, the Bird Observatory. Swallows and housemartins have arrived already! Worked in Dynogoch garden while Ernest and Col. checked the Lighthouse. The sow's not in pig.

Cold and grey on the sea; comforting to come home to a warm kitchen and fresh scones for tea.

APRIL

Bluebell time / *Amser clychau'r gôg*

One might be forgiven for thinking that the sky had come to earth in a bluebell wood on a spring morning, when the forest floor seems to be a frozen cascade of cerulean blue. The popularity of the plant is apparent in a great many ways, from the plethora of 'Bluebell' pubs to the bluebell trains that used to chug through the Oxfordshire Chilterns to allow passengers to enjoy the floral display. There is even a railway called The Bluebell Railway which runs through fives miles of woods in west Sussex. Although bluebells are to be found in many places in Europe they only occur there as individual plants: the phenomenon of blue carpets making the woodland floor look as if it's bathed in a wash of the sky is very much a British phenomenon, the plant forming a major part of the woodland herb layer. For visitors to these shores stands of bluebells can be very exciting. Bill Condry was once visited by thirty-two members of the Federation of Ontario Naturalists: 'When I led them into one of our oakwoods there were whoops of delight which puzzled me until I realised that none of them had ever seen bluebells in the mass before. They were totally enraptured by the fragrant blue sheet of flowers that spread before them away into the depths of the wood. As one of them explained, they had all heard about British bluebell woods before but never imagined such a stirring sight as this.'

We may occasionally complain about the rains which wash Wales and the fogs and mist which can obscure it, but the moist Atlantic climate suits the bluebell perfectly. In Welsh there are at least fifteen names for the bluebell, a delight in themselves, from *croeso haf*, summer welcome, through *hosanau'r gog*, cuckoo stockings to *glas y llwyn*, blue of the hedge. Bluebells enliven the Welsh woodland scene in a great many places but some of the most surprising are those on some of our Welsh islands, such as Skomer and Skokholm, where the nutrients of seabird droppings and the shelter of bracken provide a combination on which the bluebell truly thrives.

The sprung-rhythmed poet Gerard Manley Hopkins—who was educated in north Wales—loved bluebells. His view of the world was controlled by what he called 'instress and inscape' which mean, respectively, the animating energy in art, nature and God and the distinctive organic form of things. In his journal he recorded the bluebell thus:

'In the little wood/opposite the light/they stood in blackish spreads or sheddings like the spots on a snake, The heads are then like thongs and solemn in grain or grape-colour. But in the clough/through the light/they came in falls of sky-colour washing the brows and slacks of the ground with vein-blue, thickening at the double, vertical themselves and the young grass and brake fern combed vertica, but the brake struck the upright of all this with winged transomes. It was a lovely sight. The bluebells in your hand baffle you with their inscape, made to every sense: if you draw your fingers through them they are lodged and struggle/with a shock of wet heads; the long stalks rub and click and flatten to a fan on one another like your fingers themselves would when you passed the palms hard across one another, making a brittle rub and jostle like the noise of a hurdle strained by leaning against.'

Hopkins goes on to describe the 'faint honey smell and in the mouth the sweet gum.' Gummy they indeed are, with a good deal of starch stored in the roots as food. The sixteenth century herbal of William Turner enlightens us about a martial use for this stickiness: 'The boyes in Northumberland scrape the roote of the herbe and gloue their arrows and bokes with the slime that they scrape of.'

The botanist Geoffrey Grigson held the pages of a tattered journal together with bluebell glue and the book was good for a further seventeen years.

But it is their beauty that sticks in the mind. Two years after his earlier entry Gerard Manley Hopkins returned to the flower: 'May 11—Bluebells in Hodder wood, all hanging their heads one way. I caught as well as I could while my companions talked the Greek rightness of their beauty, the lovely/what people call/'gracious' bidding one to another or all one way, the level or stage or shire of colour they make hanging in the air a foot above the grass, and a notable glare the eye may abstract and sever from the blue colour/of light beating up from so many glassy heads, which like water is good to float their deeper instress in upon the mind.'

William Condry

On April 4 I saw the year's first adder asleep in the sun on a patch of dry raised ground in the heart of a reed-bed. It took me back to an early spring day thirty years ago when I met with three adders just out of hibernation in exactly that place—a suntrap sheltered from every cold wind. Two were males, beautifully patterned in silver and black. Between them, and very different because reddish-brown, was a female. I tiptoed towards this somnolent group as lightly as one can tiptoe in gumboots. At three yards distance one of the males raised his head, flickered his tongue and poured himself silently into the reeds. At two yards the other male did the same. But the female proved to be totally approachable. She lay in a coil with her head raised just off the ground and held rigidly immobile with no flickering of the tongue. She seemed more like a wood carving than a living snake. Gingerly I bent over her and after long hesitation, because I am no snake charmer, I dared to touch the top of her head very lightly. She did not react in any way. Then very softly I stroked her head. Still no sign that she was aware of my presence. Just as lightly I caressed her throat. She remained entirely indifferent. It was not until I stroked her back all the way from head to tail that she decided it was time for her to go, which she did slowly as if in a dream, leaving me grateful to have experienced such a rare encounter with the wild.

Two days later I was up on the hills in a cold north-east wind under a sky black with the threat of rain or snow. Up there, year after year, I see the year's first wheatears, always males, for they are unfailingly the leaders of the spring migration from Africa. The cock wheatear is quite colourful as bird-artists often depict him. But meet with him on the uplands and he can be an easily missed silver-grey little bird well camouflaged to live a secretive life among the silver-grey rocks all about him. Wheatear time is also ring ouzel time. And, like wheatears, ring ouzels like to be among rocks. But, unlike wheatears, ring ouzels prefer their rocks to be well upholstered with heather. They are often cliff birds, belonging to truly wild places where they can dodge out of sight as soon as they spot you, disappearing into the next gully with dashing flight. The song is often to be heard when the singer is not seen at all. And no utterance could be more unpretentious—simply one far-carrying, ringing note repeated four or five times. It has a haunting quality, especially when caught distantly on the mountain wind. The ring ouzel used to be called the mountain blackbird but its wild, withdrawing way of life separates it hugely from the familiar friendly blackbird of our gardens.

The second half of April brought the annual miracle of ever more returning birds. Despite an unwelcoming east wind the first willow warbler was singing in our garden on the twelfth, an average date, as we have noted over many years. By the fifteenth there were two, along with a chiffchaff. In the next two days we saw redstart, blackcap, pied flycatcher and plenty of swallows and sand martins. Also on schedule were the butterflies, beginning as ever with small tortoiseshell, peacock and brimstone, followed on the 26th by the first orange tip. And how envious I was that day when a friend of mine had the outrageous luck to see in our parish that rarity of rarities, a Camberwell beauty! Had it somehow come from America or had it escaped from a butterfly farm?

The 27th brought the first tree pipit singing beautifully over the peat-bog just outside our garden. Next day house martins passed over on migration, group after group every few minutes for nearly an hour, all on the same line. That day there was the garden's fifth butterfly—a speckled wood. And that night there must have been an influx of garden warblers, for next morning their songs were everywhere, often drowning the more delicate utterances of the willow warblers. On the 29th the first reed warblers were singing in our local marsh; and the month ended with the first common sandpipers—the Victorians called them summer snipe; there were two on the muddy edge of the Dyfi River, singing and making a great show of courtship display.

Patrick Dobbs

When I was twelve years old my school gave a prize to every pupil who kept a diary through the summer break. Mine was not a success, for I broke my right wrist in a fall from a horse on the second Saturday of the holiday. But I still got a prize. A cardboard certificate, embossed with the school badge and motto, and marked 'Diary—2nd class'. The habit stuck, and I've made some kind of a note of what happened to me practically every day ever since.

But in early April my style is even more laconic than usual. 'Dull. Showers. Score 179 live 8 dead' might be as much as the record had to say about all that occurred between climbing out of bed in the morning and crawling back in again at night. All inessential jobs are postponed, and there isn't any leisure time. The work is heavy and exhausting. There are bags of cake and bales of hay to be carried out to the flock. There are ewes in trouble to be brought to the gate and held by the dog, caught and man-handled into the back of the Landrover.

Welsh mountain sheep are indomitable. Their lambs are born with a tight undercoat, and I've seen them drop into the deepest and coldest puddles in the keenest east wind and get up, give a shake and start to suck in conditions where I would see an early exit from life as much the more attractive alternative. But there are some situations from which there is no escape unaided.

Coming backwards, head first, tail first, hind legs in front or just growing too big are all seriously bad ideas which need a competent shepherd to sort out. There is a phenomenon for which no flockmaster, veterinary surgeon, animal physiologist or even astrologer has ever given me any satisfying explanation —the repeated recurrence of the same malpresentation within the space of two or three days, and then not seeing it again for a couple of seasons. In the first weekend of April 1997 a whole bunch of them chose to come head first. Why? Next year perhaps I'll have as many backwards with their hocks flexed beneath them, or some other unconventional and risky route into the world. I always mark, and later cull, the ones that need assistance, so over four decades I've developed an easy lambing flock.

But for some, diligence and skill are not enough.

'Into this Universe, and Why not knowing
    Nor *Whence*, like Water willy-nilly flowing;
And out of it, as Wind along the Waste,
    I know not *Whither*, willy-nilly blowing.'

or, put more bluntly in a favourite couplet of my mother,

'Lord, he was so quickly done for
I wonder what he was begun for.'

Generally the weather makes a tough job harder still. Snow and slush, water and mud have the Landrover stranded, and the pony Max has to come to the rescue. He carries hay, feed bags and sheep, dead or alive with equal equanimity and irrepressible cheeriness. But 1997 was different. From the fourth to the sixteenth of April we enjoyed an unprecedented and unseasonable heatwave. Instead of wellingtons and waterproofs the gear was trainers and T-shirt, and if this is global warming we can't get too much of it.

As the month goes on my thoughts turn to grass. My own farm is very small, so I rent a bit extra. Grass keep is auctioned off a few fields at a time, fertilizer already spread and the crop ready to grow. On the evening of the fourteenth I was underbidder on two lots at Tynlone, two days later I was unable to attend the Rhiwe sale so I left a bid of £2,700 on a piece that went for £2,750, and at Mandinam the following week I was Mr Nearly three or four times again. Pantyscallog Sennybridge is on the red soil. I've never rented down there before, but the best of the grass looked good and so did the fencing and there's water in the river Usk however dry the summer. I gave £2,000 to graze fifteen acres until Christmas, with a couple more of rough woodland. It did me very well.

Grass is not an end product but a raw material. I buy it for the sake of my sheep, to have a fresh bite for the lambs when they come off the mountain in late summer. But in the meantime the spring growth must be put to good use, and it's no good stocking it with ewes for they would shed worm eggs all over the place to be picked up by my young and vulnerable lambs later on. I'm not a haymaker so that means grazing cattle, and I'm off to the mart to buy some.

I love the cut and thrust of the market place. I've never bet a penny on a horse or the outcome of a football match, or bought a lottery ticket, but I revel in the challenge of backing my judgement and spending thousands on livestock whose value can go down as fast as it goes up and which has a way of becoming deadstock when least expected. In years past all you had to look for were young animals with scope to improve. Nowadays you must master the intricacies of the CAP. The colour of their identification documents reveal the premium status of the cattle, and knowing their exact age is critical if you expect to make a profit. I went to Brecon fair on the twenty-fifth of April. I bought some good growing green card bullocks, and five really skinny ones that most people probably thought were too thin to survive and fatten.

But the sheep are always top of a sheep farmer's agenda, and by the end of the month all the little lambs are earmarked and pitched ready to go up the mountain. The dogs, particularly the younger ones, find baby lambs hard to handle. They run all ways at once, and when they're separated from their mothers there's chaos and confusion.

This year I tried a new trick. I injected them with cydectin, a long-acting drug to kill both intestinal worms and ticks, lice and mites. It was an expensive and time-consuming job, for the dose rate is so small and sensitive that each lamb had to be weighed individually. But if it works it will be worth it, for in summer especially sheep farmers are continually at war with an ever-present army of parasites. The farmer is on one side and the enemy on the other, with the unfortunate sheep providing the battleground in the middle.

Christine Evans

Friday 4th April
E. 4-5 backing N.E. and increasing 6-7.
Good weather (calm and gradually warming up, sunny even) for a week—we have been so busy backwards and forwards across the Sound—and weary in the evenings—the diary's been squeezed out. Haven't seen much of the island either but we've finished painting our bedroom (including staining floorboards), stairs and woodwork. Wet rot in the 'parlwr' needs proper treatment—the wooden floor gave way under Col. At least Dynogoch looks tidy from outside, 'as though somebody lives there,' as Nain, a stickler for scrubbing the steps and hand-weeding the cobbles, would say.

The shearwaters are back, Andrew told me: he's planning a systematic count of all their nests next month. And the first visitors are due at the end of next week, true to the old instinct: when winter's over 'thanne longen folk to go on pilgrimages/ And palmers for to seken straunge strondes . . .' I wonder what pilgrims to Enlli took home as proof of their successful quest instead of a palm leaf, in the days when three pilgrimages here was equivalent to one journey to Rome?

Perhaps it was less windy in the Middle Ages, but the crossing must often have been a real test of faith (cynics suggest drowning as one reason for the number of interments of saintly people.) Difficulty is a requirement of pilgrimage, of course; the currency. There are modern equivalents—the walking of long-distance footpaths, visits to Dove Cottage or Keats' grave in Rome, the blue-rinsed American woman that Peter told us about, whose life-quest is to see every kind of penguin, no expense spared—and most people who come to stay on Enlli seem to be after more than just a holiday. Bits of the island feel like Chaucer's 'halwes' (hallowed or holy places): above Bau Nant, where the pilgrims probably landed and where there might have been a large welcoming cross (the area has been called Y Groes since the first maps), and the well with its three stone steps going down into the water. But most of all for me it feels like a place to live.

I had one full day working on students' coursework (trying not to be distracted by the blackcap and thrush singing outside) and yesterday drove to Bangor for a hospital appointment. Delighted to see the trees coming into leaf on lanes sheltered from the sea, big horse chestnuts holding out bright rags, like still crumpled dragonflies' wings, to dry in the sun. B&Q was full of people buying tender fuchsias and petunias.

This afternoon, had a good walk right round the cliff to Porth Meudwy with the Robertses. We watched a kestrel quartering a gorse patch very purposefully, counted choughs and ravens, noted the skylarks singing and looked out for cetaceans (Sister Verena saw thirty or so coming round Braich-y-Pwll last week, as though perhaps they migrate into Cardigan Bay for the summer.) We found shelter from the rising wind and sat on the tip of Pen-y-Cil to enjoy the whitecaps and the rolling swell.

Now it's very cold—I think of the ram lambs Gareth sheared today so they'd look good in the early summer sale, and of tomatoes planted out in greenhouses. A wonderful but wintry sunset, the whole sky flushed before a sudden dark.

> From among a petal brightness
> the sun's pale fruit, pierced
> by a splinter of night,

ripens to peach, apricot, plum
darkening to damson, then sloe
and dissolving, spills juice
in a gush of darkness over the sky.

Tuesday 8th April
Variable, mainly southerly 2-3.
Enlli early (7.30 start): we all needed to be back for an afternoon
of 'work'. From the sea, the island looks as dry as autumn (we've
had five weeks without a spot of rain.) While Ernest went out to
lift his pots and Col. walked round the coast checking the gadgets
for his dissertation on the island's water supply (difficult this
very dry year!) I strolled up the west and through the fields,
enjoying the sun and the calling lapwings. The hayfields below
Tŷ Pella were full of heavily pregnant sheep and I lingered there
watching Tim move quietly among them, watching for the
'skypointing' of the labouring ewe. Twelve lambs, including one
set of triplets, were born in two hours. There wasn't a breath of
wind; surrounded by peaceful sheep cropping the grass or
murmuring throatily to newborn lambs, it felt a nourishing spell.

Kim and Gwydion here with eggs when we got home. She's
off to Rye for an exhibition, then to Minsmere for two weeks as
Artist in Residence. We opened a bottle of wine while I threw a
risotto together. Then another bottle.

The new moon's low on the horizon, jaunty bright, the
comet about a third of the way up the sky still looking like a
proclamation. It reminds us where we are: how small, temporary,
cosily domestic. House lights tiny as boats against all that
darkness.

Saturday 12th April
N.E. 3-4, becoming cyclonic.
All the trees are shivering, but there's no swell and the sea is
smooth enough to take the island tractor back now Col. has
finished its overhaul and respray. He and Ernest left before 7 to
bring the Sea Truck over and I went down later with a load of
sheep nuts. Greenfinches busy beside the track down to the cove.

At lunchtime, the Holyhead shellfish wholesaler phoned to say she doesn't want any crabs—the market's overloaded. It's a blow; though they only fetch about 30p a pound, it just about pays for the bait. What to do with a couple of hundredweight in the keep-pots? What's needed is some sort of processing and marketing co-operative here; prime Aberdaron or Bardsey shellfish and even ready-to-serve meals, fish soups, Thermidors and crab salad to order . . .

To Ty'n Fron for a load of four-year-old horse manure for the greenhouse—rich and crumbly as fruit cake.

Thursday 17th April
Wil at the garage reported seeing his first swallow, and summer seems here at last—trees and flowers and birdsong all the way to Glynllifon and then we had to stay in all day reading A Level folders. Glyn and I took sandwiches so we could walk as far as the amphitheatre and have lunch by the stream. The bluebells are out in Nanhoron!

On the evening news, trawlermen protesting about quota-hopping—2 tons of fish dumped in Plymouth town centre. There have to be licences and controls, especially of net sizes (world-wide plundering of the sea might be as disastrous as felling the rainforests) but we haven't found the best way of enforcing them, and I feel for all those small communities whose livelihood is being eroded away. The sea is in their blood, even though it means risking their lives every day. Factory units and business parks aren't going to be much help.

Saturday 19th April
N.E. 4-5 Cold, but no rain.
In the village to collect milk and the papers, noticed the sea sullen and heavy, no light in the breaking waves. Col. (home to type up his dissertation) went over to the island for a few hours' ploughing and I went too. The first calf born on Enlli for almost thirty years this morning—a strong bull.

Screaming gulls carve rings
of air, sky territories
over the ploughed earth.

Wednesday 23rd April
Warm and sunny. Home early after visiting first-year students
on work experience with the National Trust in Rhiw and at
Gwesty Carreg Plas, above the famous 'Whistling Sands' beach.
If I'd had the dog with me, I could have walked home over
Anelog and gone back for the car in the evening.

I disturbed some newts sunbathing in the greenhouse—on
the stream side. Hot and sweaty working in there, but all's
ready now to plant out the tomatoes.

The comet is much further west; fading now. Through
binoculars its two tails are V-shaped, like a boat's wake.

Need rain, though the mainland garden (on clay soil) looks
lush—honesty, foxgloves, blue irises and pansies and all the
fruit trees and hawthorns heavy with blossom. The aquilegia
(Granny's Bonnets) is heavy-headed with buds. There's a change
on the way if the barometer's to be believed: after weeks of
being stuck on Set Fair it must be on the move because Ernest's
doing his Father Shandyish nightly ritual again—last thing at
night as he goes up the stairs, three enquiring taps and a grave
inspection; then again as he comes down past it in the morning.

Friday 25th April
Rain at last, clearing by eight. Drove to work up the Nanhoron
valley to enjoy the trees and shine—a sense of fulfilment,
excitement, everything can really start now. The mature trees
heavy with moisture, stiff as wedding-guests in all their
finery—

AFTER RAIN, APRIL

There has been an easing:
all that was tight
loosening.

60

Sky's washed clean and shining
   like the inside of a shell.
      Buttercups gleam like ten thousand suns.
Trees with newly-coiffeured heads
   hold themselves as if for photographs
      decorously feasting matrons.

Unseen, the green core sucks and throbs.
   Patiently shed water gathers heat.
      All's ripe with moisture.

Bracken gathers
   Scatterings of shed lace

And two young sycamores with sleep-mussed hair
   begin to stir.

Tuesday 29th April
W. 5 backing northerly and decreasing 4. Blustery showers.
Awake 4.35: watched light slowly fill the room, first a grey mist
leaking in under the door and round the curtains, the silver
gleam of the mirror gradually rippling like a pond. Then the
room was brimming with light, the blackbird and (I think) a
whitethroat making outside seem mysterious woodland. I put
on my glasses and everything was ordinary again. There was
white mist winding through the willows at the bottom of the
garden, but the forecast is better. Dot, staying here after seeing
the midwife and shopping, is eager to get home, and there's a
load of lighthouse stuff in the garage—two huge boxes of
polishing cloths, chairs, a lawnmower and several gallons of
hand-cleaner (lemon-scented).

   Ernest decided to trust the forecast ('the sun will kill the
wind'), so they left about 10.

   Transplanting Little Gem lettuces, listening to *Kaleidoscope*, I
heard Ned Thomas talking about the new translation of R.S.'s
autobiographical writing. The best bit of the day, an absorbed
interlude, my hands busy in warm earth, the noise of bees in the

apple blossom and the Berberis (they love the tiny curled-up yellow flowers), sun on my back and on the faces of blue pansies, surrounded by the smell of growing.

MAY

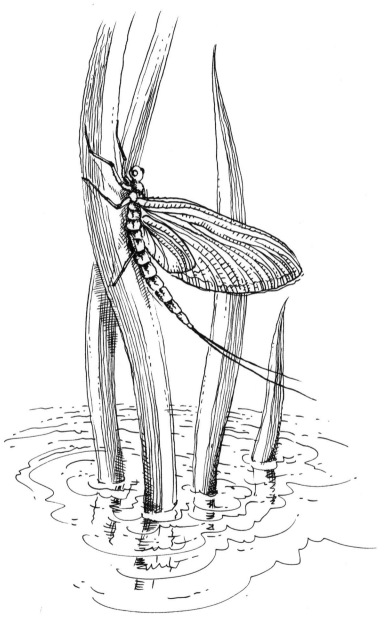

Mayfly Dances/*Dawns Gwybed Mai*

You might be forgiven for not noticing mayflies other than when the adult males of some species swarm over still or running water, a dizzy roundel of the air, a spiralling insect tango on the smallest of airwaves. They are not strong fliers and before a swarm can assemble calm air is a prerequisite. The merest hint of a breeze may scatter individual insects which then drop to the ground. Occasionally they can get caught up in a wind and very large numbers have been seen being swept out to sea. I have seen such kamikaze squadrons drifting out over the silky sands of Cefn Sidan near Llanelli where sea bass no doubt welcome them with open mouths.

Freshwaterside scenes are this month much enlivened by these insects—often in gargantuan numbers—which take their name from the month, but, once airborne, never live that long.

Mayflies have the briefest of brief lives, a fact reflected in the name of the order of insects to which they belong—Ephemeroptera, from the Greek *ephemeros*, which means living for a day. The mouth parts of the winged insects are lost, so they take no food whatsoever during the aerial stage of their lives. The winged adults only survive for between an hour and a couple of days, although there is some compensation in that the insect is unique in having two flying stages—the first, the subimago, later moulting into the fully formed, if instantly doomed, adult. This phenomenon isn't found anywhere else among modern insects although ancestral insects may have done the same. There is still some debate as to the whys and wherefores of this phenomenon—it might allow the tails and legs to grow to a length which they couldn't otherwise attain, the insects needing long tails for stability in flight and long legs for holding on to the female as they mate.

This inability to fly strongly probably accounts for the habit of swarming. Females, carrying the weight of eggs, are even weaker fliers than the males and so their chances of finding a mate are greatly improved if all the males gather in one place, in an aerial discotheque where the dances are stately and busy at the same time: anti-gravity gavottes. The males often position themselves relative to a marker, such as a small bush, over which the swarm gathers and maintains position.

The overall shape of a swarm may appear to be fairly constant. As anyone who has watched a large gathering of birds such as, say dunlin at winter, flashing light and dark, flying wing to wing, separating the individuals with the eye is a sure course to madness. But there are those who have studied mayflies swarming and apparently (to them!) the individuals within a swarm are changing places continuously.

A male near the bottom of the swarm flies quite rapidly upwards, in some species twisting and turning around other males, and touching them with his legs. When he reaches the top of the swarm the male then generally drifts downwards, often with wings outstretched, dropping down like a spindly parachute. The front legs and tails are curved upwards until, when he is near the bottom, he turns and flies upwards again.

At intervals the female flies into the swarm, perhaps attracted by the wing movements. The number of females entering a swarm at any time seems to be very small. Often there is only one. In general she keeps to the top and with a bit of patience it is possible to spot the female at the top of the dizzying mass.

Much of what we know about mayflies comes from the observations of anglers rather than the examinations of entomologists. Fishermen know mayflies as upwing flies. They feature on the menu card for so many fish that a book such as *The Anglers Entomology* is pretty much entirely devoted to mayflies at various stages of life.

The names given by fishermen to mayflies, fake and real, are a found poem: the Pale Watery, the Iron Blue, the Medium Olive and the Dusky Yellow Streak. There is the Little Claret and the Red or Small Spinner, the Drake Mackerel, the Sherry Spinner and all manner of duns, the Sepia Dun, the Claret Dun and Purple Dun. Duns become spinners; that is, the subimagos become imagos and fly into their brief days, their doomed and dizzying dances, dances of death on a river's breath.

On a sun-filled day in May, where better to walk than along the sea cliffs whose natural rock gardens are now at their best? Cushions of white sea campion and scurvy-grass, pink thrift and yellow lady's fingers which some call kidney vetch— they adorn the rocks for mile after mile. On my walk there today I came eventually to something that is rare along this coast of Cardigan Bay—a patch of woodland, not a mere scrub of blackthorn but a genuine oakwood clinging bravely to existence right above the sea where the Atlantic tempests are at their fiercest and the salt in the air most concentrated. Though these oaks are stunted (the tallest not more than twice my height) they are unquestionably old and probably the descendants of oaks that have occupied this site ever since oaks first got here after the ice age. As I sat in their shade eating my lunch I speculated not only about the history of these trees but about the other plants all round me: how long have they too been there, defying the sea winds and the salt? Here they all are— bluebells, stitchworts, sanicles, dog's mercury, wood sorrel— decidedly the flora of oakwoods yet flourishing on sea cliffs. And adding to the authentic oakwood atmosphere are the birds—tree pipits, chaffinches and willow warblers, their songs strange to hear mingling with the groans and growls of shags and guillemots nesting on ledges a few feet below. Sitting there among those tangled primaeval trees and listening to the beating of the sea, I had a feeling of true wilderness that is now so rare in the world. I thought back to an October day some years ago in an autumn that was full of falling acorns everywhere. When I saw thousands of them showering into our garden I wondered about the oakwoods out on the sea cliffs. Would even those unpromising trees be loaded with acorns? I decided to go and see. On a day wild with winds and squalls of rain and a roaring sea below, I groped among the oak dwarfs searching the ground for acorns. I did not have to look long. For although very few of the trees had produced any at all, some of them had, especially the tallest at the top of the wood and farthest from the sea. I found that the majority of the acorns had fallen outside the woodland fence on to sheep pasture where they had no hope of survival. So I gathered as many as I could and then followed the fence until I reached a clearing in the oaks and there I scattered my acorns. No doubt most were soon eaten by mice or voles but I like to think that one or two managed to germinate and become the oaks of the next millennium.

* * *

May 9 was a mainly sunny day threatening showers that did not happen. A friend and I walked from Eisteddfa Gurig to the top of Plynlimon and ate our lunch in the lee of the cairn piled up at great cost of energy by the people of the Bronze Age about whose life up there we know so little. As we sat there in warm sunshine we watched three little birds only thirty yards away running about the turf amongst the scattered stones. They were dotterels—those beautiful little plovers whose unique migrations take them from mountain-top to mountain-top from south to north in spring and back again in autumn. We strolled for a mile or two along the summit (is there a finer ridge walk in all Wales?) grateful to hear the singing of skylarks in these days when they have become so scarce in many districts. We saw a few wheatears and for a couple of minutes there was a kite circling above us. In the clear air the views were magnificent nearly all round and especially to the east where the Breidden Hills at Welshpool stood up sharply and where we could even make out details of the Shropshire plain beyond. The panorama was wide all the way from the Berwyn in the north-east to Radnor Forest, the Brecon Beacons, the Carmarthen Van and Presely in the south. Cardigan Bay shone silver all across to Bardsey Island. Every height in Meirionnydd was easily recognisable—Tarren y Gesail, Cader Idris, Rhobell Fawr, Arenig, Aran Fawddwy and the rest. Only the hills further north were darkened by haze and there was no trace at all of

Snowdon or Moel Hebog. But days of clarity all round the compass are rare indeed.

Now it is late in May and I write this sitting on a mossy boulder botanising the lazy way. I am looking up through binoculars at a wealth of plants covering the face of a cliff. It is not a mountain cliff nor a sea cliff but one that is a few miles inland and only a few hundred feet above sea level. So I am not looking at alpines nor at plants that love the kiss of the sea winds. What plants should we expect to find on such a crag, given that its rocks are moderately rich in lime and broken up into many damp cracks and ledges just perfect for most plants to get their roots into? The answer is mainly the plants of woodlands, for woods and cool, damp cliffs can have much in common from a plant's point of view. What I see, as my binoculars search along the ledges, are primroses, bluebells, red campion, violets and yellow sprays of wood spurge. And I know that when some of these have faded, the summer will bring the purple-pink flowers of orpine; the yellow of rock stonecrop (*Sedum forsterianum*) that so loves Wales; the white of ox-eye daisies; along with hawkweeds, marjoram and valerian. I could list others but now I am interrupted by the arrival of a peregrine. He is standing on the highest ledge complaining bitterly about my being there so near to his nest. And as I always feel most uncomfortable when wailed at by indignant peregrines I must depart forthwith.

Patrick Dobbs

It is the first of May and it's polling day, and for the first time in my life I don't vote for the Labour candidate in an election to public office. Historically of course farmers have done better with a Labour government than a Conservative one, but the legacy of Tom Williams can't last for ever, and when we are told that the financial institutions of the City of London, who should

69

be shaking in their shoes at the prospect of a Labour victory, would be quite happy with a Blair government it's time to reassess my position. The job of a democratic socialist party, especially after eighteen years of Tory control, should be to comfort the afflicted and to afflict the comfortable, and the modernised Labour party seems all set to do just the opposite. In the past few years I've been told at Labour party meetings all over the constituency that nothing, nothing at all, is more important than success at this election. Well, I reckon there are worse things to lose than an election, such as your own sense of integrity and purpose. All the same, it does feel strange to put my cross in a different square.

There's been a disaster at Pantyscallog, and I have to go over to salvage what I can. One of my Brecon bullocks has taken a tumble and crashed into the rocky bed of the river Usk. He's lying on a shoal of gravel towards the further bank, his forelegs horribly swollen and cuts on his quarters and flanks. Experience suggests that the best course is to cut my losses—the knacker man is cheaper than the vet. Inevitably he was one of the best, very expensive. One thing is certain: I can't leave him here. I encourage him to scramble through the shallow water, more on his knees than his feet, to my side of the river. I leave him lying as comfortably as I can, and offer him a wodge of the best hay I can find.

Back home and I'm on the telephone. He's going to cost me a lot of money whatever I do. He cannot be legally moved to an abattoir even if I could get him into a trailer, and if I shoot him where he lies I will have to hire a digger to dispose of his rather large carcase. All the vet can suggest is painkillers and prayer. It's the best option from the few dismal alternatives, and I take him hay every day and see he gets enough to drink and doesn't lie permanently on the same side. The swellings increase alarmingly, then slowly, very slowly, they begin to go down. Eventually he shuffles along after the herd. His legs return to a somewhat more orthodox shape. He has lost a lot of condition and all his youthful bloom. [He makes a pretty good recovery, not in weeks but in months.]

The Worldly Hope men set their Hearts upon
Turns Ashes—or it prospers; and anon,
Like Snow upon the Desert's dusty face,
Lighting a little hour or two—is gone.'

In the summer of 1996, with the cattle trade crazy with Mad Cow disease and depending more on luck than judgement, I bought a load of mares and foals. I spent many years in the horse trade, and though I hadn't lost my eye I had lost my familiarity with the ups and downs of the market and most of my contacts had died—many of them literally. I thought they would pay better than bullocks. I could not have been more wrong. Some I did sell before the winter, but I was still left with a yearling filly and three mares that would have to be broken and ridden regularly if I was to get real money for them.

The old cavesson came down from its hook and I was out in the paddock lungeing them round, walk, trot and stop to the word of command then long-reining them up the lane and round about the place as I had done years ago when I used to break colts by the lorry load. Then it's screw up my courage, slip on their backs and hope they are sufficiently confident and good-natured not to allow panic or resentment to get the better of them. Soon I was riding them up to the church or along the track to Llyn y Fan; one very good, one pretty good and the other—let's say, a bit difficult.

We had a cold spell in the early part of the month. I had to re-kindle the kitchen fire, and the early summer sun was broken with showers. A wet May is generally a prosperous one, but the weeds grew as fast as the grass and they had to be cut back in the youngest plantations. I've planted thousands of ash and oaks, rowans and birch trees, even a few beech, wild apples and cherries over the last few years, and I'm not going to see them overgrown with cocksfoot, nettles, docks and thistles.

I'm often up at four and out with the scythe by five o'clock. I love the early mornings. This is the year of the hares. I've never seen leverets so big so early. There are at least two distinct families, one in Tirbwch beyond the flat field and the other over by the Gellionnen boundary. The young ones are foolish things, and show themselves in the open as though they had nothing to fear from anyone or anything. I think they are living dangerously. When I need a change from weeding I fetch one of the young mares from her field. They are all shod, and I ride any of them on the mountain.

Now the sheep need driving out, for they graze in competition with other flocks, some brought from as far away as Llangadog. I let the dogs run wide, and hope they don't scuttle beneath the feet of my still inexperienced cob. The rays of the early sun, still low in the sky, dapple the mountainside with light and shade, for every rock has its shadow, each stream and pool reflects the dawn. I look at these familiar slopes practically every day of my life and walk or ride up here on most of them, but always I see something new, a different angle of the horizon, a fresh colour in the rock or a brighter yellow on the gorse. I sometimes wonder, if my work didn't bring me this way, if I would actually ride for recreation or just walk over the hill for the hell of it.

Christine Evans

Thursday 1st May
Foghorn sounding all night and we woke to a submerged landscape: cold, dank, though the radio kept telling us it was 24 degrees and last night's tv weather chart was all bright yellow with only a few cotton-wool smudges over the Isle of Man. Mildly annoying to be blithely informed that everybody is at risk of sunburn when we can't see further than the first hedge; feel I should tell somebody. We've just had the driest 24 months since records began apparently.

After supper, down to vote. The old school, busy with laughter and sociable exchanges, had a slightly surprised feel.

Late evening, the air grew warmer. I took the dog for a scamper round Stelyg—could hear several foxes over the skyline in the scrub down in Porth Llanllawen, probably cubs' contact calls. So there was one vixen left, at least.

Friday 2nd May
'A new dawn' was how the radio woke us at 6.45. The birds had already finished singing. 'And what will you remember of the last six weeks, the build-up to perhaps the most momentous election of our times?' In this backwater (and safe Plaid seat) I haven't seen a single campaigner, except on t.v.; and I wouldn't want it any different. I drove slowly to work enjoying the greens and the brash gold of gorse everywhere, sign of a dry summer, they say. And 'a hot May makes a fat churchyard' while ' a cold May is kindly/and fills the barns finely' (my father remembered this from his childhood around Monmouth.)

Col. and I walked the smooth green paths on the headland down to Maen Melyn Llŷn, a squat stump, supposedly a Neolithic standing stone that from the sea looks like a thumb hitching a lift to Ireland. As the sun went down it changed colour—flushed pink—the only 'melyn' about it the brilliant yolk-yellow lichen.

Hale-Bopp is far away now and fading—paler than the stars and more diffuse. Through binoculars the core is still clear, the tail streaming straight up behind it. From the first week of March to the first week of May it was a wonder we grew accustomed to. I shall miss it.

Tuesday 6th May
N. or N.W. 6-7, occasionally gale 8.
Last night sounded like winter and we woke to a sky full of fine white flakes that were not apple blossom but snow, the skylight opaque as though buried. None of it stuck here, though it was bad elsewhere in Wales—15 centimetres in Rhuthun—and it was bitterly cold—3 degrees this morning. Such a contrast for the Bank Holiday visitors—scorching 25 degrees when they arrive and blizzards as they drive home. All day yesterday the wind rose, trees lashed and witch-rags of torn black polythene (bale-wrappings) flapped wildly on wire fences. Landing

73

lobsters, Ernest had to cut the ropes of the keep-pots; the wind was suddenly so strong it was dragging him across the bay. A thing he's never had to do before.

Sorted out a paraffin heater for the greenhouse to save the tomato plants from frost.

Wednesday May 7th
S.W. 6-8. Squally showers.
Evening reading at Tŷ Newydd—Kim came as driver, and it was the 'Poetry and Painting' course which always attracts interesting people. One of the painters has camped on Bychestyn and heard shearwaters there, as I have—and Gwydion—none of the serious ornithologists seem to believe that they may nest on the mainland. Last time I read at one of these courses the late drive home was spectacular—'full moon and foxcrossed', beside a brilliantly silver sea. Tonight was miserable, the car buffeted by vicious gusts and hail driving straight at us as though we were on warp drive through an asteroid belt . . . Home to a sleeping house at 1 a.m. Even the dog's greeting was half-hearted, but Ernest roused enough to tell me that Trinity House had reported the lighthouse 'off normal' again, only the emergency light working and a need to get out there a.s.a.p. May be a chance tomorrow as the centre of the depression will be right over us (which usually means a headache for me.)

Thursday 15th May
The first silage cut—several farms in the eighteen miles between here and Pwllheli seem to have synchronised their programme. I love to see the patterns in the fields like huge green runes.

Monday 19th May
N.N.E. 3 or 4.
On the way to college, intrigued by Lewis Wolpert on *Start the Week* wondering whether the universe might be a living organism, self-replicating through one of the one billion billion black holes they estimate. I was reminded of the Nobel winner

74

Richard Feynman's remark that a sense of the surreal is necessary in astro-physics; as a child he had a hard time deciding whether to be a comedian or a scientist.

> Does Time end in a black hole
> or is it endlessly rebooted
> in a Big Bang that spawns
> another million galaxies?

So I was late for my first lecture.

Ernest got soaked at the Lighthouse—the Trinity House ship Mermaid was unloading generator fuel by helicopter. Tried the first early potatoes from the garden; small but tasty.

Tuesday 20th May
N 3 backing N.W. 4-5.
The centre of the depression moving right over us—low clouds, very oppressive. Reports of several mini-tornadoes and a funnel cloud between Manchester and Liverpool. I was busy all afternoon taking phone calls—apparently yesterday diesel got sprayed on the lighthouse garden from a perforated pipe and it's being treated by the media as a major 'Oil Spill on Wildlife Island' incident. Ernest had to go straight back to check out the damage—only superficial but smelly, so he'll have to get a crew together to dig out all the contaminated soil first thing tomorrow. It's a feeder pipe that's been perforated in over-enthusiastic forking by some of the Observatory staff who grow potatoes in the old garden.

Sunday 25th May
Weekend in Llanrhaeadr, at Tŷ'r Helyg, with the Roberts family. I liked the cupped richness of the Vale of Clwyd, but not its busy road. We walked on a gorse hill high above the Abbey of St. Beuno, Hopkins country. Looking out over the many textures of farmland and woods and towns, patterns of sun and shade, ringed by ancient hillforts (Moel Fenlli among them) was very peaceful, though there were fewer birds than here. To

Mold to see *The English Patient* in the evening—wonderful patterns of dunes and water-worn sandstone caves. And today, back over the mountains to Llangollen—another contrast, suburban gardens, picnic by the big, rushing river—followed by Keith Bowen's exhibition *Among the Amish*. Huge, vivid pictures: images of the sun's warmth in rich greens and oranges of crops and the bright bay horses balanced by the cold blues and stark white of winter in this Pennsylvania community that turns its back on modern technology. A feast for the eye.

And now begins the holiday week—we've planned for Enlli every day (to finish painting,) but daren't go to stay in case we can't get off, and Col. is in the middle of Finals at Aberystwyth.

JUNE

A Swift Month/*Mis y Wennol Ddu*

Some of my halcyon years were spent in Newtown, Montgomeryshire, where part of the joy was owed not to the kingfisher which gives its old name, the halcyon, to such happy times but to other birds entirely—to swifts.

Newtown is an old market town which has a clock as its centrepoint, which, in high summer becomes a marker post for dizzy legions of swifts as they race around the town. On summer evenings their scimitar shapes scythe along the river Severn, above which the air is at times quite *sooty* with insects, which explains the numerous plops of rising trout and the excited trill of the swifts. Listening to their screeching with the seeming exultation of it all, what Ted Hughes called materializing 'at the tip of a long scream of needle', it seemed little wonder that one name for these supreme flyers was the 'devil bird', demonically weaving an invisible tangle of flightpaths over the old woollen warehouses of the older parts of town. For these are urban birds—tied in more intimately to the life of town and city than any other species in Wales—which explains their presence in high numbers in cities such as Cardiff and Swansea. There are also a few cliff-nesting colonies of swifts in Wales, at Fall Bay and Mewslade on south Gower and in the fissured limestone of south Pembrokeshire.

I remember one day a bird flying through my office window and skidding to an ignominious halt on my desk, where its utter helplessness on land was as apparent as can be. Swifts' legs are weak from lack of use—seldom doing much more than a bit of clinging onto walls, nothing too strenuous—and there was no way this deskbound bird was going to get airborne from a standing start. So the best act of kindness was to let it compose itself a little before tossing it out the window through which it came! It was a heart-stopping moment, not knowing whether it would plummet to the ground or not, but luckily it hurtled away without so much as a goodbye screech.

Swifts do everything on the wing, opening the great gape of their mouths so that they become flying insect traps. All they have to do is 'open wide' and unfortunate flies and doomed moths find themselves inside. Their diet also includes a good many small spiders, dispersing in the sky attached to their long gossamer threads. Such food is very much at the mercy of the vagaries of the weather, being much more plentiful in warm rather than windy and wet weather, and perhaps more than any other species the swift is sensitive to weather conditions. Warm, dry summers suit it well.

Swifts occasionally mate on the wing—often following a spectacular aerial chase—whilst birds not involved in incubating eggs or brooding young actually sleep on the wing, drifting up on the rising thermals of the evening and sleeping for short spells before animated bursts of wing-flapping help them gain some more height.

Swifts also fight. There is one famous account of a battle, watched in a tower in Oxford, where a swift entering an occupied nest fought for a total of five and three quarter hours. Pairs of swifts are sometimes found on the ground, alive and interlocked after some scrap or other.

Their stay with us is short—one is almost tempted to say nothing more than a swift visit! Theirs is one of the briefest sojourns by any of our summer visitors: only the cuckoo's stay is shorter. They arrive in late April, though more usually and in greater numbers in early May, and by the middle of August swifts have started their enormous aerial trek to southern Africa. This year's birds become totally independent of their parents once they have left the nest, and leave the country as soon as they have fledged, followed in a few days by their parents.

The Welsh poet John Ormond watched swifts in Italy. In his poem 'Evening in the Square' he describes, with an energy to match their wheeling flight, the business of being swifts:

> The swifts are invisibly mending the sky
> Where last night's wind tore it to pieces,
> Stitching, delirious with light labour,
> High on it, with dizzy double-daring
> Done in twos. Such works a tall order.

Dizzy they may be, but oh how they grace and excite the summertime skies! Invisible menders! Fancy.

William Condry

Every few years I like to go off in June to check on a favourite plant of mine called spignel. It grows in the semi-uplands around Dolgellau and Llanuwchllyn and it is rare. It is an enigmatic plant. It belongs emphatically to Scotland and the north of England and is so isolated here in north Wales that there has to be a suspicion that it was planted here by man. But why bring it here? Sniff its leaves and you may get a clue. They smell strongly of the herb garden and therefore hint at monastic associations. So it may not be just a coincidence that it has been found not far from ancient trackways and that there was a medieval hospice only a mile from one of its sites. Known to science as *Meum athamanticum*, it is a small, white-flowered umbellifer with many short, fine leaves. Edward Lhuyd, source of so much of our knowledge of mountain plants, got acquainted with spignel in Meirionnydd in 1682. So historically it would be a great loss if it were to die out here. But the auguries are not good: under the combined onslaught of excessive sheep-grazing and the ploughing and reseeding of old pastures, spignel could easily disappear.

* * *

What could be more beautiful than a great spread of cotton-grass shining white in the sunshine of late June? I walk through this forest of graceful, knee-high seed-heads to a wide stretch of sphagnum mosses where my gumboots sink dangerously into quaking bog. Here the sundews are busy, tiny plants occupied night and day catching and killing insects on their gummy leaves and, astonishingly, digesting them. Today I find a creature as large as a wall butterfly has been caught. I come to a thicket of sallows and look carefully for the eggs of eyed hawkmoths stuck singly on the underside of the leaves but I find none, though in other years I have found them on that bush. But so many plants and animals go through enormous fluctuations in numbers whose explanation we can only guess at. Past the sallows I come to where the bog is purple, mauve and white with the massed blooms of hundreds of heath spotted orchids. Then I go over the railway bank and on to the estuary where far away I can see several families of shelducks, mergansers and Canada geese drifting slowly westwards on the falling tide. In the oakwood on the way home I note how dark-green the leaves have become and how much fewer are the bird voices compared with only a week ago. Inescapably June, though it is the peak of the year, has its forlorn side. It begins full of song but ends with very little and it is a sad thought that not until next April shall we again hear the cheerful voices of warblers, redstarts, tree pipits, pied flycatchers and other migrants. For compensation we can turn to butterflies, provided the sun is shining. They have done well so far this year and just now small coppers, small heaths, painted ladies, walls and common blues are plentiful and we have meadow browns, ringlets, gatekeepers and large and small skippers to look forward to. Whenever the sun is hot the horseflies bite hotly too. Frequently it rains. In a word it is midsummer.

* * *

June 29. A good day. A friend drove me across Montgomeryshire to see the floral treasures of the north-east Wales limestone where it reaches its southern limit at Llanymynech Hill. It was because of birds not plants that long ago I first became aware of Llanymynech. In the early fifties a well-known birdwatcher, J. H. Owen, was a gifted nest-finder who, in his retirement, devoted all his hours every spring to investigating the breeding statistic of some of the local birds, especially robins and spotted flycatchers. His results were impressive. In 1951, for instance, he not only found 127 flycatcher nests but also monitored their successes and failures so painstakingly that at the end of the season he could report that the number of eggs the flycatchers incubated was 362, that 50 were deserted or removed during incubation, that 20 were addled, that 292 chicks hatched, that 54 did not outlive the nestling stage, that 238 reached the juvenile stage, that male birds helped with the building of some nests, that there was much inexplicable desertion of nests and that many deserted nests were returned to several weeks later.

On the day of our visit we were guided up the hill by Marjorie Wainwright who knows more than anyone about the flora of Montgomeryshire and who showed us many lovely flowers as we made our way from the old limestone quarry up to the golf course. I was relieved to see that since my last visit years ago a great quantity of old man's beard had been removed because it had been rampaging everywhere and smothering some very desirable plants. This wild clematis, so abundant on limestone, is something we hardly ever see in our limeless, western district. Its other common name is traveller's joy but it certainly is not conservationists' joy any more than that smotherer on acid soils, wild rhododendron. From our day on this charming hill I brought back memories of many beautiful plants—bee orchids at perfection, twayblades of immense stature, greater butterfly orchids, rockroses, small scabious, huge hartstongues, houndstongue, black bryony and many other lime-lovers we see little of where I live. We were also shown two rare whitebeams —*Sorbus anglica* and *S. latifolia*. By far the commonest butterfly was the small heath which I was pleased to see is just as at home on limestone as it is on acid moorlands. There were many painted ladies for it is a summer of painted ladies everywhere, sometimes in amazing numbers. Though we tried to keep an eye on the birds (not easy when you're botanising) we saw no spotted flycatchers at all for they have become almost scarce in recent years. I thought how unhappy J. H. Owen would have been had he lived to see this flycatcher apparently going the way of the red-backed shrike which he remembered as common on the hill in the early decades of this century.

Patrick Dobbs

I sold one of my mares. She was the best of them: small ears, deep-bodied, short legs, wide chest, tremendous quarters and, an unusual quality for a Welsh cob, a really good shoulder so you didn't feel as though you were going to slide over her ears when she took you down a steep bank. She was quiet, active and strong. What more could you ask?

'So did this horse excel a common one,
In shape, in courage, colour, pace and bone.

Round-hoof'd, short-jointed, fetlocks shag and long,
Broad breast, full eye, small head, and nostril wide,
High crest, short ears, straight legs and passing strong,
Thin mane, thick tail, broad buttock, tender hide . . .'

William Shakespeare, *Venus and Adonis*

I sold her at Llanybydder horse sale and I didn't enjoy it, but I have more at home and I know that if I keep Vicky the others will just grow fatter and idler with disuse. The money, though better than anything else in the ring that day, bore little relation to the hours of work and bales of hay that had gone into her. But who, in these days of the quad bike, the estate car and the hatchback, wants a really good shepherding pony or a useful family cob?

On the eleventh of June I took my Landrover into Hay-on-Wye for a service, and sped off in my 'courtesy car' for a couple of hours in Hereford. I love Hereford on a Wednesday, with its market full of pigs and calves, older cattle and sheep, farm produce of every kind, plants and poultry. Especially poultry. There is a fascination about the trade in ferrets (yes, they sell those, and rabbits too), Cayuga ducks and elderly Rhode Island hens. Fortunately this morning I show great restraint, and only buy four goslings for twelve pounds the lot and eight 'mixed chicks' at twenty pence each.

As a poultry farmer I have an unparalleled record of unsuccess. If they escape the eye of magpies and ravens when they are very small they generally end up in the belly of a fox or a polecat before they reach maturity. This time I penned them under the canopy of an old sheep trailer, and didn't let them wander out until they were of an age to look after themselves. The poultry industry is now so high-tech and intensive that it is difficult to buy a suitably balanced ration that isn't laced with prophylactic antibiotics to protect the little birds against the diseases of stress and overcrowding. All right, I suppose, if they are going to end up in a supermarket freezer cabinet, but as I'm going to eat my geese and chickens myself I really don't want them drugged to the eyeballs before they've even fallen ill.

Thieves came to Llanddeusant one Friday. They took my chainsaw, a saddle, two electric drills, a lamp, a nice wooden box with drawers full of nails and such odds and ends as they could quickly snatch. The insurance company paid compensation, but insisted I renew the locks and bolt the windows. I needed no second telling, for being broken into is quite astonishingly disturbing and unpleasant as well as being expensive. So several fine sunny days in June, great for working in the fields, were spent round the yard fixing weldmesh over the windows and sinking mortice locks into doors and frames.

For half a lifetime I never even bothered to secure the outside doors, and would leave the keys in my motor at the mart in case anyone wanted to move it out of the way. Now I am bolted, barred and battened down and record the number of every transit van that passes by. They blame drugs, unemployment and the M4.

There were unwelcome visitors to the horses' field as well, for tiny flies or mites spread the misery of sweet itch in midsummer and the pony Max seems to get it every year. He rubs his neck and he rubs his backside until he's sore. I bring him in three or four times a week to dress his mane and tail. I have used a permethrin, organo-phosphorus, compound to keep the flies and mites away, but I prefer the relatively benign benzyl benzoate which has an anaesthetic action. Neither treatment is wholly satisfactory.

I bought Max in winter when his condition didn't show, although I should have known better after many many years in the horse trade, for his mane was cut short, a proper old horse copers' trick. But he was such a smart cob, and I was desperate to get one to pull my plantation waggon—a glorious four-wheeled carriage that came all the way from Brazil. I bought it not in South America but at a farm sale at the foot of the Llanllwni mountain. I thought one of my bigger cobs would be suitable, but when I got it home I realised it must have been designed for a mule or a big Spanish jack of the stamp I used to work with in Guyana back in the 1950s. Max goes really well in it, and takes food out for the sheep in winter as well.

By the twentieth of June I was pretty sick myself: 'flu caught off a long forgotten Norwegian acquaintance who stopped by on her first visit to Llyn y Fan for twenty years. We gossiped, shared a cup of coffee, and she left me with her cold that was more than a cold and it stuck with me until well into July. To add to my troubles the weather was cold too, and on the twenty-fifth of the month I actually lit my fire for a couple of days.

The sheep were too wet to shear. I gathered most of them off the mountain on the fifteenth and found another twenty the following day, but it took me a fortnight to get them all in. On some days I was too ill to go out. Then I'd go to work again too soon, and on the day after I'd be worse than I was the day before. Not a satisfactory or enjoyable way to run a farm.

Christine Evans

Monday 2nd June
Windy (easterly) but dry and bright for the first A Level English paper. A relief.
Elderflowers, strawberries, dogroses, swifts (*gwennol ddu*) that sleep on the wing so that when they arrive they are all alertness, shiny with quickness. And need to be; they'll be away again in

86

the middle of August, the most intense of our birds' family-raising.

Thursday 5th June
N.E. becoming S.E 5 or 6, Thundery showers.
Barometer dropping like a stone, Ernest says this morning. Final revision session with students—on the Wife of Bath and R.S. Thomas (strange bedfellows!) but we all felt headachey and listless—low barometric pressure, I think: weather does affect people.

Saturday 7th June
S.W. 5-6, 7 at times. Rain.
Disappointing weather for Gillian Clarke's 60th birthday party at Tŷ Newydd but it cleared in the afternoon and the gardens were radiant after the rain. The smell of steamy grass in the marquee was like camping and the small-time agricultural shows of my childhood.

Being invited to contribute a poem to a Blodeuwedd anthology set me thinking about the way the story's images might still be alive; the idea of a woman of flowers, created purely for gratification (though today we probably wouldn't choose oak, broom and meadowsweet). As amoral as an animal. I'm very tempted by the metamorphosis into owl—imagine her looking in a mirror, feathers thickening about her like snow, burying the human features . . .

> feather-face
> in a body with the power
> at last, to hurt

and in the end, it's not punishment, but freedom

> out of the pattern
> out of the circle
> out of the mirror
> into the freeing dark.

But I shall probably try a contemporary version.

Sunday 8th June

Ernest and Col. went to see a windmill that's for sale second-hand (thinking of Enlli.) Mairwen and family came over and we walked on Mynydd Mawr in the wind, but the sea was too rough and the tide too high to go down to Ffynnon Fair.

In afternoon, brilliant sun so picked elderflowers for *Bod Isaf Elderflower Cordia*l:

50 flowerheads, as free from stalk as possible
4 lemons, sliced
4 lbs sugar
4 oz citric acid
5 pints boiling water
1 Campden tablet for bottling (to stop fermentation)
A lidded container, preferably plastic

Pour the boiling water over the flowers, lemons, sugar and citric acid. Stir well and make sure the sugar has dissolved. Leave for 5 days. Strain . Add one crushed Campden tablet to the liquid and bottle.

Dilute about 1-10.

This makes a concentrated syrupy cordial which will keep for a year. Refreshing in summer with sparkling water, ice and lemon (or white wine or even gin or vodka!) it's equally good as a hot winter drink

Tuesday 10th June

This has been fledgling week—the escallonia hedges of our garden have been thick with young chaffinches, blackbirds, robins and sparrows, the air busy with wings and urgent calls.

Before the second English exam, picnicked on Pengarn above college with some of the second year students—my last lot. Hawthorn blossom in the sun almost cloying.

Marking exam papers in evening when Nicoli phoned from her home on Puget Sound near Seattle—she'd just been warned off by the nesting swans Franklin and Eleanor, who were disturbed and abandoned their eggs last year while she was staying here.

Friday 13th June

My last day in college; now the teaching's over, my contract has finished, though I'll have papers to mark, reports and UCAS assessments to complete. As I was clearing my room (25 years teaching makes for an accumulation of paper) several students popped in with gifts and cards—chocolates from James, an aromatic candle from Angharad, Lea with a lovely bunch of scarlet Sweet Williams.

Strained and bottled the elderflower cordial to t.v. programme about Clyde Holmes, poet and landscape painter who lives in Cwm Hesgyn on that wild land above Bala. I saw some of his work in Aber last year and found it a very moving programme, more about the loneliness of living with a dedicated artist than about him. And remoteness: those people who come to Enlli to be 'solitary' could be truly isolated up there.

> With the children grown up and gone
> You think of the winters, wind-howl
> in the chimney, snow islanding them . . .

Too bleak for me to go on imagining.

Saturday 14th June
N.E. 4.

Rita and John called, collecting Dafydd after a fortnight at the Bird Observatory; they brought kale and a variety of white flower plants and walked round the garden which is looking increasingly jumbled—foxgloves 4 feet high among the lettuces, blue geranium among the bush tomatoes and courgettes, red cabbage and black kale in the herbaceous bit. 'Is that a sunflower in your vegetable patch?' asked John but I don't think he really disapproved; it's going to be really showy, almost 7' now and the flowerhead just swelling above velvety greyish leaves. I like the way what was a boggy rectangle of rough field is turning into four different rooms.

Tuesday 17th June
Hot and sunny. Staying overnight in Pontrhydfendigaid with Hazel and John on their smallholding above Tregaron Bog where J has been working for twenty years or so, since they left Skomer. A patchwork of small fields, conifers, stone walls, the sharpness in the air that speaks of altitude; heather growing on the verges. I enjoy driving down, watching the topography change. South of Aberystwyth it's so much more padded, softly rounded, 'essentially feminine' as Gillian Clarke has it in *Letter from A Far Country.*

I catch up with their news. John is to retire from CCW this summer; the kites have had another successful season; their sheep flock have done well. I tell them of changes on Enlli, of the imminence of Tim and Dot's baby and the reason for my trip, to meet the potential granny and whisk her back before the helicopter's called.

Leaning out of my bedroom window I sense something missing in the night quiet here, though there's a tawny owl calling. After a moment I realise it's the ever-present murmuring of the sea that's lacking.

Wednesday 18th June
Met Daphne and loaded up with a few years' worth of babygear at WAC, the Welsh Agricultural College that's become part of the University called WIRS—the Welsh Institute of Rural Studies. It was sunny and calm as we set off but 'Get your foot down,' urged Col. when we stopped to phone; 'the weather's changing.' Sure enough we met rain in Dolgellau, and a south-east wind getting up as we came over Trawsfynydd. It was a frustratingly slow journey behind caravans, heavy-laden lorries and tourists with nowhere special to go. Tim had come over to fetch his mum and they headed out of Porth into thick mist. By the time he phoned to say they'd arrived safely, it was blowing hard, with driving rain.

Saturday 21st June
N.E. 5-7, perhaps gale 8, continuous rain.
Heavy rain all day—50 mm in 24 hours according to Gwilym Garregfawr who monitors the weather station. Selwyn rang, complaining of the cold in Melbourne—their winter solstice and it's 13 degrees (here it's been 10 and 11 even during the day.) It's his third consecutive winter: he was teaching in China, then came to Coleg Harlech last October, before going home in March.

People going to stay on Enlli have been delayed again; a miserable start to their holiday.

Monday 30th June
N.E. 5-6, gusting 7 on exposed coasts.
Another low pressure swirl moving over us. 'The wettest June this century' say the newscasters. Is the weather really all extremes or is it simply the way the statistics are used?

Floods in Scotland—many people round Elgin evacuated. The air's like autumn rather than midsummer—only 10 degrees and the smell of smashed wet vegetation. I'm packed and ready to go to stay on the island as soon as Dot's had the baby and the weather's settled. There's still fruit to pick when it's dry enough, and freeze or preserve. I made 16 pounds of green gooseberry jam today.

A peregrine was perched on the telegraph wires watching pigeons in the front field with a proprietorial air. About forty of them, feeding on the battered corn. He must have decided they weren't quite fat enough and took off casually in the direction of Parwyd. I suppose he was one of the nesting pair. (I once saw one perched like an oversized robin on the spade handle in the garden.)

JULY

Hedgehog Days/*Dyddiau'r draenog*

I was reading a newspaper on an evening in late July. Some early-riser pipistrelle bats were hyperactively chasing insects around the cottage where I was staying, while the sibilant hiss of my pal Gordon's scythe cutting its way through long grass was almost enough to lull me to sleep. Gordon is prone to accidents—on one famous occasion he was knocked over by an ambulance—and when I heard a yelp coming from outside I presumed the worst. Fortunately when I got to the other side of the shoulder-high bramble jungle he was staring at a young hedgehog which lay unharmed but looking immensely vulnerable near the scythe blade. Safely transferred to a cardboard box, Harry, as we promptly named him, turned two grown men into fussing matrons, armed with the only fact we knew, that hedgehogs have fleas, and scratching at the very word. Luckily we found out just in time that cow's milk is dangerously over-nutritious to a baby hedgehog so by the time our twenty-four-hour-long ministrations were over, and we had handed Harry into the care of Mrs Tiddeywinks at the local hedgehog sanctuary, our young charge had actually gained an ounce or two. A later report confirmed that Harry was spikily well and about to be set free.

The hedgehog is an ancient species which was bumbling around long before mammoths and sabre-toothed tigers. It is widespread in Wales, avoiding only watery places and is one of those few species which has found, by snuffling around, that suburban gardens offer a new habitat to favour and savour.

Reading the very engaging book by Pat Morris called *Hedgehogs* I was bowled over to learn that the largest hedgehog she had found was over four and a half pounds and that a specimen this big might have as many as 7,500 spines on its body.

Hedgehogs are unique in one respect and that is a curious phenomenon called self-anointing where the animal generates oodles of frothy saliva which it then flicks with its tongue over its back and sides so that it looks as if it has just been through a car wash. The best theory, so far, about this curious act is that it's a scent thing, with a substance contained in the saliva which works much as do certain kinds of air freshener—wafted from pockets between the spine and the fur to mark out territory or attract a mate.

As you can imagine, the mating of such spiny creatures is not an easy business and many females, despite having mated, fail to get pregnant. I'll let you imagine things.

There will be many people who assume that the hedgehog that appears in the garden to feast on bread and milk is the same hedgehog, night after night, showing its faithfulness but often it's a case of many different animals passing through. They can display a prodigious appetite, able to eat up to ten per cent of their own body weight in a sitting, like a human adult slurping up seventeen pounds of muesli at a go!

Most people will know that hedgehogs hibernate but fewer will know that this is not so much a long sleep as a device for storing energy rather than a rest after a summer and autumn of snuffling and pootling around. And of course, in the winter, as the temperature drops and the earth hardens, the beetles and worms which feature on the hedgehog diet sheet become more difficult to find so the energy used in finding them can soon outweigh the energy released after eating them.

During the hibernation period the hedgehog gradually burns up the fat it has stored during the summer and autumn, which at the start of the hibernation process can be as much as a third of the animal's body weight. Hedgehogs do wake up during this period, not for long but fairly regularly, about once a week. The occasional individual might even go for a walk before slowing down again and returning to its *hibernaculum*, the proper name for the winter nest.

This it builds on the ground, with an architecture of leaves which it carries to the chosen site. Once the hedgehog has gathered enough leaves it burrows and shuffles itself deeper and deeper into the pile. This habit is responsible for the dangers of Guy Fawkes night when the hedgehog might have built its hibernaculum in the middle of a bonfire.

There was a new moon last night and I sit on the railway bank this morning to watch a great tide fill the estuary. From here I can see where, four miles west at Aberdyfi, white sea water is pouring in over the bar; but it will be a while yet before the estuary's wide, dry sands will be submerged. Time passes and the creeks begin to fill. The salt water arrives sparkling and clear but it turns brown and mud-laden as it is forced bubbling and hissing up the channels. It is full of life, this water that brings its regular refreshment to the estuary's multitudes of creatures and plants. It teems with plankton and sometimes with sand eels and the tiny fish the locals call 'brit' which are said to be the young of sprats, herrings and others. I cannot see these fishlets in the turgid water but the Sandwich terns can. Half-way across the estuary, where the tide flows quickly inland, the gleaming white terns are circling and diving where the brit are evidently most concentrated. In a creek just below me there is a splashing of much larger fish that swim with their backs out of the water and through binoculars I can see they are dark-green and beautifully patterned. These are bass, powerful hunters which, like the terns, are after the brit. They move up the estuary and are followed by other surface splashers—a herd of grey mullets. As vegetarians they are no threat to other fish but no doubt the brit retreat before them all the same.

The scene now changes rapidly. Looking round I see grey water overspilling everywhere from the maze of winding creeks. Mud flats, sand banks and vast green fields of tall spartina grass are all vanishing. For another twenty minutes I watch the gracefully buoyant terns diving into the streaming tide and coming out with bright little fish. Now the estuary has become a tapering arm of the sea, six miles long and two miles wide at its mouth. A warm sunlit stillness settles everywhere. We have reached the moment of full tide. But that elusive instant has already passed. A brood of shelducks, floating in mid-estuary, is drifting gently seawards. The play is nearly over.

July is a good time to go out to the islands off the western extremities of Pembrokeshire but it is best to go early in the month, before the seabirds begin to disperse. I write this on Skomer, more blessed with birds than any Welsh island, home to great colonies of puffins, guillemots, razorbills, kittiwakes, shearwaters, petrels and others. And surely it can't be long before gannets will be added to the list as they begin to overpopulate neighbouring Grassholm? To come to Skomer is to set foot on an island that people down the ages have used for farming, fishing, rabbiting and catching seabirds but which has at last gone back to the wild as all such islands should. It is an uneven, cliff-surrounded plateau high above the sea, pimpled with tors of igneous rock, much wind-tormented and virtually treeless. Its name was given to it by the Vikings who, over a thousand years ago, held power round the coast of Wales. How interesting it would be if we could discover what they thought of the place and what birds and plants then flourished here. Were the cliffs in those days wailing with rank above rank of kittiwakes and groaning with multitudes of razorbills and guillemots, as they do today? Did puffins hold their silent assemblies among the sea-pinks? Were there choughs, peregrines, buzzards? Did seals breed on the beaches? Were the bank voles by then already a distinct island race of superior size? And were the nights alive with caterwauling shearwaters and purring storm petrels?

Come to Skomer in May and you will find some slopes so deep in bluebells they can be seen from the mainland two miles away. Were they just as multitudinous in the Viking time? And was bracken there then, vast jungles of it, hiding the nests of throngs of gulls and the rare short-eared owls? And what about the people who lived on Skomer a thousand years before the Vikings and whose walls still outline the little Iron Age fields? What was Skomer like then? We will never know; but what we can be sure about is that Skomer never has been a place for easy living and has always belonged to the gales, the salty spume and the streaming tides.

Suppose, as you arrive at Martin's Haven, that the worst happens, the winds are unkind and, though you have come from afar, you cannot cross to the lovely island. You need not despair. There is a flower-rich walk along the mainland cliffs from the deer park past Gateholm Island to the popular sands of Marloes. You should come in May or June to see the cliff-top flowers at their best: sea campion, thrift, scurvy-grass, kidney vetch, birdsfoot trefoil and others. You will also see strange specimens of common broom which have opted to lie flat on the ground rather than form bushes. Have they given up the unequal struggle against the gales? For lovers of past things there are traces of the Iron Age along this shore: just before you come opposite Gateholm you will see the multiple banks of a promontory fort; and on the flat top of Gateholm, mostly hidden in the vegetation, are the hut remains of what may have been a monastic settlement of early Christian times. The cliffs around Marloes Sands are dear to geologists: the fossils here exhibit a splendid range of the succession of rocks of the Silurian Age.

A special memory I have of this part of the coast is of a bottle-nosed dolphin. These small whales are wonderful to see rolling through the waves but normally keep well away from the shore. But there was a summer a few years ago when one decided to spend a season with humanity in Martin's Haven. Day after day it was there playing among the dinghies and the people or following the boats across to Skomer. Such jolly fraternising would be more understandable in seals. For often, as you walk along the shore, a seal will keep up with you in the water only a few yards away, watching you without fear and simply, it seems, in a spirit of inquiry. Dolphins are different: they belong to the deep and do not come ashore unless distressed; and they have nothing to do with people apart from those eccentric individual dolphins which—and they turn up worldwide—suddenly choose to frolic with the human family. But why?

Patrick Dobbs

I t's the first of July and not a sheep has been sheared. I used to love shearing. It was a thing I could do, but it's a long time since I went round the farms for one shilling and threepence a head plus a good meal and a hot bath at the end of the day. As I turn back the years in my journal I see the incredible daily tally that I once caught, clipped, pitched, rolled and often dosed, single-handed.

> 'Whether at Naishápúr or Babylon,
> Whether the Cup with sweet of bitter run,
> The Wine of Life keeps oozing drop by drop,
> The Leaves of Life keep falling one by one.'

Now I'm shopping for someone else's meal. I splash out on extravagant hams and cold meat already cooked, cheeses, lettuces, eggs, pickles and dozens of brown buns—all things I can lay out on the table early in the day and cover with a cloth so it's ready any time at a moment's notice. I boil up some blackcurrants to go with cream and ice-cream. Itinerant shearers are wild spirits, like birds. Give them plenty of nice things to eat and they'll be back again next year.

The lean-to is swept clean, for dirt, damp, dust and dead vegetation are the enemies of a clean fleece. I organise gates and hurdles and the hay in the silo is covered with polythene so it won't tangle up in the fibres. The first wool sheet, a giant sack to hold some forty fleeces, is suspended between two girders and a dozen more are ready to hand. The Wool Board labels and grease-proof string, a pair of scissors and a kitchen knife all go in a bucket nearby.

The day before we're due to go, the fourth of July to be exact and a couple of weeks later than usual, I take nineteen ewes and all the rams into the shed. I clip them with my old machine, just to confirm what I know already—I don't really need a shearing gang. I could still do them myself if I wanted to. It's just that I have other things to do with my limited time. Why I chose to do the rams I can't imagine, for they are twice the size and four times the weight of ewes. Next year I expect I'll keep my hand in on a bunch of yearlings.

You can't start shearing very early in the morning, as it's a good deal simpler to dry a fleece on the ewe than after it's been taken off. Mike comes to help for the day, and we get the flock to the roadside pens by half past nine. The shearers, all New Zealanders but only travelling from Builth Wells this morning, arrive at about ten o'clock. They take half an hour to set up their machines in the shade of the lean-to, while I separate the first eighty or so from their lambs and run them down to the catching pens. The shearers turn up their radio, oil their combs and cutters and off they go.

Fortunately Mike, wrapping fleeces and throwing them over the silo wall for me to pack in the sheets whenever I get a few minutes to spare, has the same taste in music as the antipodeans. I find the noise of the sheep, the blare of Radio Two and the drone of the motors extraordinarily disagreeable, and try to have everything arranged so I don't spend too much time in the shed. I sort out more ewes. I fix hurdles and gates so the shorn sheep, bleating and bewildered, run out into the field to rejoin their lambs with a minimum of disruption and hassle. I maintain an endless supply of orange squash and keep busy with a broom, fork and shovel. I keep my eyes open for any sign of injuries, mastitis or maggots that may be uncovered as the fleeces fall away.

Dinner time. Perhaps New Zealanders live in wooden shanties or mud huts, for they always gaze in disbelief at the stone walls and oak beams that hold my house together. Over the years I've renovated it out of all recognition, the walls and floors are hardly ever damp and the roof never leaks even when it's raining. The men enjoy their meal and really appreciate it. This year they've just finished a stint on a big estate in central England where only the farmer, his family and his dogs were allowed round the table and the shearers had to eat sitting on the step outside. We have a brief conversation about the Japanese crayfish market, deer farming and computers then get back to work.

101

By ten o'clock that night, with the yard lights blazing and the midges biting, it's all over. The whole flock bar a few stragglers is shorn and the equipment back in the transit. We go indoors to enjoy a prejudiced post-mortem on some historic encounter between Wales and the All Blacks over tea, beer and the left-overs of dinner. The next morning I'm as tired and stiff as if I'd had a hard day shearing myself. I inject sheep and wean the first ten lambs, taking them down to Pantyscallog in the back of the Landrover when I go to check the cattle. I pack the last few fleeces into the sheets, press them down hard and sew them up and tie on the labels.

That evening I go to the Court Leet at Cross Inn. Graziers on the common from the Amman and Swansea valleys and Breconshire meet the Llanddeusant, Gwynfe and Myddfai people to reclaim strays and try to identify torn earmarks and faded pitch. We go into the bar, and a local solicitor, the steward of the manor, takes us through a feudal rigmarole to dispose of forfeit sheep. A sworn jury appoints valuers, who advise on the price to be paid by the beadle for stray sheep he has kept for twelve months unclaimed. The Court deals with any matter relating to the common, trespass by tourists and the military, minor improvements to gates, grids and communal pens, whether and when the mountain should be cleared to dip or inject the sheep and usually discusses correspondence from the Brecon Beacons National Park who now own the freehold. It makes for a long evening, but it's best to keep in touch with what is or might be going on.

Later in the month I take more lambs to Pantyscallog to wean them far from the sight or sound of their mothers. The break is final and complete, although when the ewe lambs return to the mountain as yearlings they are often seen grazing as a family group. As the weather turns hot and sultry flies become a problem. The sheep must be gathered from the fields to spray them with Vetrazine against a maggot strike, but on the high mountain they are usually safe enough.

On the eleventh of July I load five Pantyscallog steers into my trailer for Sennybridge mart. They've earned a premium by keeping them a couple of months while their identity cards change from green to blue, and they show a handsome increase in market price as well. You can't beat farming when it's going really well.

Christine Evans

Saturday 5th July Dynogoch, Enlli
Variable, 2 to 3 Fog banks.
Crossed in fog—watching the island grow on the radar screen, ourselves a blip ringed with concentric quarter-mile circles. In mid-Sound, the boat broke through into a sudden clear patch—astonishingly brilliant light and heat for a few moments, then plunged back into clammy grey. A single guillemot welcomed us to the east side, crossing back and forwards over the boat as if trying to divert us; perhaps it had a chick in the water. Last week in Porth Meudwy I watched an oystercatcher repeatedly screaming and dive-bombing a herring-gull until it was forced to fly off, dropping the young bird it had snatched— quite dead by then.

No-one in the Cafn, no bird noise even: a warm bubble silently stretching to let us in.

Cut the grass round the house and got busy painting the spare bedroom. Hot in the afternoon (25/6 degrees) but the mist came down again and is pressed thick against the window as I write. I walked down through the lapwing fields after checking with Andrew, the Warden, that there were no nests to disturb— they've failed to breed for a second year, despite the attempt to restore the tillage and bring back cattle. What lapwings need is boggy, broken ground in early spring with crops growing up quickly for cover so that predators—crows, ravens, blackbacks and here, most of all, the peregrine—don't get the chicks. An indication of how common they used to be is a casual reference in Gilbert White's *Natural History of Selborne*: 'Lapwings' eggs at the poulterer's, May 8th' (but that was in 1769). On most islands seabirds' eggs used to be harvested, but Sudne Ward-Jones who grew up here in the second decade of the century told me quite indignantly: 'we had plenty of hens and ducks.' In the 70s somebody did try swapping pickled herring-gulls' eggs for beer in the Ship in Aberdaron, but the novelty wore off.

Thursday July 10th Dynogoch

Calm grey morning. Ernest out round the pots before I wake, despite the echoing stairs and back door that needs to be banged shut. Hearing the boat's engines, I looked at the clock—6.20. Did a couple of hours digging (extending the cultivated area of this neglected garden) while it was cool. Sowed more lettuce, radish, peas. A young robin watched from about two feet away, and I wasted time watching six bees dance. I couldn't tell what was being said, but they all suddenly took off and disappeared.

Helped Col. load some woolsacks to take across tomorrow—they're hoping it'll be calm enough to bring the Welsh Black bull for his 'holiday'.

Mid-afternoon: walked over Pen Cristin—dry sweet air wafting the scent of coumarin from the fields Col. has 'topped'—and then down to wallow in the pool in Traeth Ffynnon. Salt prickles on the skin as it dries quickly in the sun's heat. There's a tired sigh as the tide sucks out, then a quickening whisper and shush! as it returns.

Only Esther and I were in the Cafn when Tim—and family—arrived. There should have been a proper welcome for Iestyn, just eight days old, but we were all more concerned to keep him out of the sun. His first bumpy ride on the trailer!

Noson Lawen in the evening in Hendy. Merêd, in fine form, had already composed an *englyn*.

CROESO I IESTYN I ENLLI, GORFF 10, 1997

O erwau llawer garwach—eu dadwrdd,
A'u didaw ddynionach
I ynys sy'n dirionach
Ei hafan, daeth baban bach.

104

Ac i Iestyn rhaid llunio—geiriau teg,
Geiriau twym o groeso,
A mynnwn oll ddymuno
Hardd o fyd lle cerdda fo.

Merêd (Dr. Meredydd Evans)
Ar ran pawb mewn noson lawen yn Hendy.

A WELCOME TO IESTYN TO BARDSEY, JULY 10, 1997

From harsher acres, loud
with the babble of mankind
to an island's gentler haven
has come a newborn child.

And for Iestyn words need shaping
words of welcoming warmth
and what each one of us is wishing;
a lovely world where he may walk.

Merêd
On behalf of everyone at the Hendy *noson lawen.*

Wednesday July 17th
Warm but overcast. Lighthouse duty in the morning. Walked
back round the west, seeing the gullies at low water weed-
draped and dripping, great slabs of rock split or tossed in heaps
by the casual power of the sea.

In the ruins of the 18th century house, Tŷ Newydd, Esther
and the other students on archaeology course discovered more
bones—the skeletons of 5 children, all together (buried in a pit,
they think) but lying north-south, unlike the others they have
found there. (The usual alignment for a Christian burial is west
—east, of course—to face the Lord when the Last Trump sounds.)

Reading in the School 7.30—a responsive audience (had to
carry benches from the Observatory so everyone could sit).
When I read 'A green lane lined with meadowsweet' this year, I
can point out how the plant is creeping back now sheep grazing
is controlled.

105

Friday July 19th
N. 3 or 4, becoming variable 2.
10.30 a.m. Sitting by the upstairs window—bright sun and shiny sea, a stiff northerly rustling in the escallonia hedges and banging on the front door now and then. The bay is vivid blue and smooth; *Bugail Enlli* moored, unmoving, Ernest bringing *William J* in slowly from lifting the lobster pots. Across the Narrows though the sea is simmering, a brilliant silver crawling and churning to a pale horizon. The hay meadows look calm enough, spread out in a patchwork below, but Tim's potatoes are shivering and the spring barley is tossing like a miniature bright green sea.

Esther's just run up to change after a swim, she thought the Cafn would be deserted but 'I couldn't have met more people if I'd tried': all the archaeology students, a boatload of fifteen day visitors, then Iain and Gareth over for sheep-dipping. They've brought the Nefyn Health Visitor to check the baby—15 days old today. She makes me a coffee and tells me the news: early boat tomorrow (7 a.m.). We'll have to be down there to say goodbye, and greet the new arrivals: Esther's parents coming to the Observatory, all the Trust houses are full and the Friends of Cardigan Bay dolphin-watchers are staying in the lighthouse and aboard their ketch *Pendragon*. The weather looks settled all week: Col. will probably mow the hayfields later. And am I coming to help put the sheep through the race?

I always find it hard to write when I'm here, even just keeping this diary. There's always something to be doing; every corner of the island is inviting on a day like this, and every bit of the day, and I feel as though I 'fit'. I don't need to keep hold of the experiences minute by minute. On the mainland, however busy, I write at night; here, the lighthouse hypnotises me into deep sleep, instantly. It's an effort to separate the details: the island is a place I know so well that at times I am absorbed in its 'completed fullness' (*llonydd gorffenedig*, a phrase of R. Williams Parry I memorised for its own fullness), the wholeness of so many different things in balance.

There's a sense here of other lives, generations of people like flocks of migrating birds, the bay flecked with ghost-sails. 'The

106

life of the Spirit seems to have sunk into the ground' in Archbishop Gwilym's words; 'a thin place' is what Donald Allchin calls it. Sr Seraphina has told me how she feels at home with the resonances of prayer (I imagine this as a sort of gardening on deep soil, enriched by previous generations of tenders.)

> This is where, like the birds, I return:
> a garden where I too belong
> for a time, where I have built
> between the apple tree and warm stone
> ringed by the sea's breath
> part sanctuary, part frontier
> where, busy
> among whispers of older lives
> from cockerel crow to sealsong
> at midnight
> in each fivefold lighthouse flash
> I am like breath in an instrument
> part of all this.

Tuesday July 22nd
Variable 2 or 3.
Mist clearing—the top of the lighthouse an island in a creamy sea.

Dolphin day—5 or 6 Risso's sighted on the east side, but *Pendragon* is in Pwllheli for a repair to her steering so Megan co-opted Col. from cutting the hay to take her out in his boat. The dolphins had disappeared by then.

Last sowings of lettuce, radish, peas, summer cabbages planted out. In the afternoon Ernest and Urien (Meg's eleven-year-old son who'd been joshed about his rod festooned with hooks of all sizes) came back with a load of pollack, wrasse and *morlas* (coalfish) to share out round the island. PHJ and Linda came for a meal—crab, lamb, new potatoes and veg from the garden, my version of tiramisu—only the last (and the wine) not island produce.

Thursday 24th July
Long-eared owl in Cristin withy.

Another magically calm evening. Walking back from the football (islanders against the rest) with the Roberts family, a large meteorite made a fiery-orange flowering in the north-eastern sky, swinging across above Cristin as though it might have been something that mattered, not just a burning stone blinking once against the dark. Only Rita and I saw it: the others were picking a way through the stones. I see this as a fitting symbol for our first month's freedom.

Saturday 26th July
S.E 5-6, veering N.W. and moderating 5. Fog. Frequent heavy showers.
Rough, wet and foggy. The *Irene Mary* set off early to collect the Observatory visitors but the Trust boat has been cancelled for 48 hours.

Thursday 31st July
Dark and overcast at 5 a.m. Heavy rain started shortly after 7, continuing intermittently all day, with the foghorn sounding mournfully. A performance of The Tempest is planned for tonight at Plas-yn-Rhiw, outdoors. I expect it will have to be cancelled.

My reading in the School was made special by having Russian Orthodox Bishop Basil and Sister Seraphina in the audience. Went well—there was a satisfying rightness about some of the lines in context; they seemed to go home, like feeling nails going true into place—if that's not too grim an analogy in a Christian context; what I have in mind is the making aspect.

Afterwards Ernest and I walked down to Carreg where, over a glass or three of red wine, Eleri Lewis Jones told me about her stay on Floreana, one of the inhabited Galapagos Islands. Absorbing as a novel.

AUGUST

Shearwater nights / *Nosweithiau adar drycin Manaw*

A summer night on one of our shearwater islands in Wales is an experience unlike any other. I was a callow fourteen-year-old when I first encountered these small and distant relatives of the albatross for the first time, and it was a night not only to remember but to savour: the invisible hurtling shapes and that cry, a cry best described by that lyrical poet of shearwater studies, R. M. Lockley: 'Like the crow of a throaty rooster whose head is chopped off before the last long note has fairly begun.' This gurgling sound mixed in with eerie burbling and cackles delivered in wild, orgiastic bursts gives rise to one of the local names for the bird: 'cocklolly' in Pembrokeshire.

Half the world's population of these extraordinary birds nest on the islands of Skokholm, Skomer, Bardsey and—a recently established and burgeoning colony—Ramsey island. Indeed there is a famous account (famous, that is, if you read the Viking sagas) which tells of a Viking fleet moored off the coast of the Calf of Man, an islet located south of the Isle of Man, destined for a battle near Dublin. They were attacked by what they took to be ravens which fled in the morning. It is more than likely that the Norsemen defended themselves with sword and shield against shearwaters, ghostly legions of them.

I once came up against a defence mechanism that the Manx shearwater employs against human beings when I spent a perfectly idyllic summer working on Bardsey island—undeniably the happiest summer of my days. At night, when I was out with a torch finding the birds to ring them, they would occasionally spray me with a fishy mulch. Now there wasn't a shower or a bath available to lowly assistant wardens like myself and so by the end of my island shift it was not only a case of it being a hot summer, the drought of '76, but also, personally speaking, a very high summer!

To get home I had to catch the train from Pwllheli to Aberystwyth and despite the fact that the train was full of holidaymakers I had a princely journey, with a carriage all to myself. The ticket inspector grimaced when I presented him with my ticket along with a waft of essence of old herring. He pointedly opened the windows as he moved to the next carriage.

Ronald Lockley, writing in *The Times* of 28 June 1952, recounts how a shearwater, taken to America and released by the manager of the Boston Symphony Orchestra on the morning of 3 June, was back in its Skokholm burrow in the early hours of 16 June, ten hours before news of the release, brought by the much slower postal service, had reached the island! The shearwater had covered 5150 km in 12½ days, achieving an average speed of 17 kilometres per hour. This suggests that the birds head straight for home with no dallying.

Manx shearwaters travel great distances, with birds from the Welsh colonies ranging across the entire Irish Sea, St. George's channel and the British channel to feed. Some even go as far away as the Bay of Biscay, mainly heading after herring. But those are just short hops for shearwaters, considering the enormous loop which takes them across the southern Atlantic Ocean to spend the winter off the coast of Uruguay, Brazil and Argentina before returning to Wales to breed once again. As they fly they seem hardly to flap their wings, shearing the waves, their wings outstretched in level flight using wind currents set up by the wave troughs and crests.

Before they return to the islands at night, they gather in great congregations or rafts, settling on the sea, waiting for the cover of night. On land these are ungainly birds, their legs set far back so that a shuffle is the most dignified way of describing their procession.

They nest in burrows, often taking advantage of old rabbit holes. On moonlit nights big gulls stand sentinel at the holes and in the morning the only evidence of the nocturnal carnage is the picked-over breastbones and wings of the unfortunate cocklollies.

Those evening gatherings, those raftings, were beautifully described by Lockley, a careful naturalist and a much neglected but wonderful writer. Come with him in a small boat drifting out to open water as the sun disappears:

112

'As the sun slowly sank behind the lonely island of Grassholm the great rafts of shearwaters would rise and skim in circles and figures of eight, waiting restlessly for darkness.

The flocks would swing as one being, their white breasts now a silver flash in the sun's last rays, and then, as their dark upper parts were simultaneously presented, they showed velvet-black on the grey-black sea. They would settle on the water again, so that from the island cliffs a mile distant we could barely discern the united host—it was merely a cloud shadow, a black streak like a puff of wind or a vein of the tide on calm water.'

I cannot hope to improve on Lockley's words, so I'll leave it at that. But if you can, spend a night on a shearwater island. It is an experience to match a rainforest dawn.

William Condry

Sunday, August 4. Today I went through the heat on a pilgrimage to the Cistercian abbey of Strata Florida which is in mid-Wales and was carefully sited to be isolated from the rest of the medieval world by the Cambrian Mountains in the east and the great bog of Tregaron in the west. My pilgrimage was not a religious one. It is just that from time to time I have a whim to follow a mile or two in the steps of dear old George Borrow who came this way in November, 1854, on his walk from north to south Wales. All the way he was in great spirits and tip-top physical form, striding along, as he put it: 'with a bounding and elastic step and I never remember to have felt more happy and cheerful.' In such a mood he reaches Strata Florida, inspects the abbey ruins which he thinks 'solemn and impressive'; and in the churchyard he finds an ancient yew which he hopes marks the burial place of the great medieval lyricist, Dafydd ap Gwilym. 'Taking off my hat,' he writes in *Wild Wales*, 'I knelt down and kissed its root.' I like to picture that scene—silver-haired Borrow; he never passed over the chance of a bit of drama. He had come to Wales to write an amusing book and I can hear him chuckling as he knelt to kiss that root.

At Strata Florida I was luckier than George with the weather. His day was 'sullen'. Mine was radiant and the spacious churchyard was dancing with butterflies, mostly meadow browns with a few large skippers, tortoiseshells and red admirals. Had I been there next day I would probably have seen a great fluttering of painted ladies because on that Monday they were suddenly all over the district in huge numbers. This was their second appearance. They had first arrived at the end of May and by June 13 they were in unbelievable multitudes. A friend of mine spoke of 'literally thousands' visible at one time along the western margins of Borth Bog. Numbers remained high for two or three weeks but on July 26 I wrote in my diary: 'All the painted ladies of last month have completely vanished and I have looked in vain for caterpillars.' But now, on August 5, here they were again; or rather here was a new wave of them, all in perfectly fresh colouring, as if newly hatched. [They remained common until late September and the last one my diary remembers was in our garden along with a comma on October 13].

*　*　*

A hill rises steeply at the back of our house and a seat at the top gives a wide view of the Dyfi estuary and its many ducks, geese, waders, gulls and herons. Occasionally a passing kite, peregrine or hen harrier. Even an osprey sometimes. But today I have butterflies on my mind. The sky is azure, the sunshine gentle and the breeze no more than a caress. And from the top of the rocky ridge I am watching purple hairstreaks as they flutter among the crowns of oaks which, though old, are dwarfed by the stony soil and the gales off the sea. In most woods the purple hairstreak can be difficult to observe because it keeps so devoutly to the tree-tops, hardly ever coming down to visit flowers. But from this seat at oak-top level the hairstreaks are easy to see when every few minutes they fly up out of the leaves, chase each other about, then quickly settle again; and I can clearly catch the purple flash of their wings as they take the sunlight. It is only in July and August that I see them. For the rest of the year I know nothing about them except what the books have told me: how, for instance, they lay their eggs near the leaf buds of the oaks; how the eggs remain there all through the winter; how next spring the tiny larvae eat into the buds; how, when fully fed, the larvae crawl all the way down the trunk of the tree (a real odyssey for so tiny a creature) to pupate in the ground and in so doing are, according to one author, eaten in huge numbers. But that is too dismal a thought for such a delicious summer morning with these lively little butterflies playing so happily in their trees.

* * *

There was a time when I regularly led parties round our local oakwoods telling them about the birds. Not that we saw all that many because they were mostly hidden in the leaves; but all around us we heard their songs and calls. Most people knew the common birds well enough: blackbird, song thrush, chaffinch, great tit, robin, hedge sparrow, wren. But few were familiar with the redstart's short tremulous phrase; or with the two quite different songs of the wood warbler; or the gentle utterances of the pied flycatcher; or how to distinguish the rich voices of blackcap and garden warbler (which quite often defeated me too). These woodland excursions were a delight of late April, May and early June; but from mid-June things began to get difficult as, one after another, the birds went quickly out of song. By July near silence had settled on the woods and in August it was even worse. The birds were still there, most of them, but they had largely taken to a life in the tree-tops and had joined together in mixed parties of tits, warblers, creepers and nuthatches that moved through the woods in almost total silence and were very hard to see properly.

115

Now, near the end of August, the quiet continues except that chiffchaffs are starting to sing again, not with anything like the enthusiasm of spring but fitfully, a few half-hearted snatches of notes here and there, as the birds wander through the trees, snapping at flies as they go. Woodpigeons too are singing again and undulating over the woods in courtship flight, for they often have a second or third family in late summer or autumn. But the noisiest birds this month have been, as in every August, the young buzzards that are a few weeks out of the nest. Their plaintive wailing has been almost incessant as they followed their parents round, demanding to be fed. They are slow in becoming independent but by September most of them will be off to seek their fortune elsewhere.

Patrick Dobbs

I took my wool into Brecon on the fourth of August. I used to wait for a lorry to collect it, and sometimes that would be well into winter. Wool is a perishable product. It suffers terribly if it gets wet, and the lanolin can dry out if you leave it lying about for long enough. It gets in the way. Besides, the Wool Board pays a modest fee if you haul it to the warehouse yourself.

The sacks measure about eight feet by four, and if you stuff them full, push the fleeces down hard, they can weigh pretty near a hundred kilograms. Loading them up is no light undertaking. If they're not packed tight the job is even harder, because you can't roll them along or lever them up into a tidy stack. Somehow I manage to fit them all into my big trailer, but it's a bit like squeezing peas into a pod or sausages into a tin.

Raw wool doesn't make much compared to what we get from lambs, breeding sheep and subsidies, but I like to do the best I can with it. I see it weighed, and within minutes the grader sorts my fleeces according to their type and quality. He works fast, making quick decisions between the bin coded for Welsh Cast, Red Kempy and Light Grey Welsh or more curiously Swaledale and Dalesbred Grey, although of course to a wool grader the names describe the wool not the sheep. Every year the Wool Board awards a trophy to the Champion Wool Producer of the Year, and two Llanddeusant graziers have won it in the 1990s. My own standards are nowhere near theirs, but their achievement reflects well on the whole parish.

Later that week I take another bunch of store cattle to Sennybridge mart, and one of them I have to take back to Pantyscallog immediately because his documentation isn't right. Cross continentals they are, Belgian Blues, and supposed to have double muscles on their backsides although these ones aren't the best. I suppose they're just the thing for the hamburger and cellophane-wrapped trade, but to put in my freezer I fancy the taste and texture of a Welsh Black or Hereford cross, and I've made sure I've got the very thing. He's black with a white face, I've got him on a red card with all the premia claimed, and as soon as the sale's over I take him to Billy George in Talgarth. He's dead by the time I've parked the Landrover. I take the liver, heart and lungs home with me for me and the dogs and arrange to have him hung in the cool room for three weeks. I can never understand why beef is sold before it's ready. It takes a couple of years or more to grow a decent bullock, so why can't the greedy butchers wait an extra week or two before putting it in the shop?

I bought my steers carefully and at the right price, so although some do better than others even the worst do well. The skinny animals from Brecon, treated for worms and lice before they're even turned out of the trailer into the field, are unrecognisable, and I sell them all fat. Every one except the casualty leaves a good margin, and they pay all the grass rent so I reckon I get the sheep grazing for nothing.

Back at Blaenau I've been keeping a few cows and calves for a friend, but I want more and decide to buy some heifers. They should clear up the pastures that are a little overgrown after the heavy rain of June and early July and leave a bit of profit as well. As they carry no premia and don't have to be kept for a two month retention period they can be cashed at any time, which makes them simpler than steers, and they will be company for my injured bullock who has still got swollen ankles and is hobbling. So I go to Llandovery and spend between ninety pence and a pound a kilo on thirteen Charolais crosses, costing me not far short of five thousand pounds. Not, as it turned out, a good day's work. I went to the sheepdog trials at Llanwrtyd the same day, and I didn't do any good there either.

I enjoy an hour or two at the dog trials, although in recent years I've hardly won anything. Back in the 1960s I had two good dogs, one of them very good, and between them they pretty well won enough to pay for the petrol. Nowadays competitors seem to take it more seriously, there are fewer of them and you are up against the same dogs and handlers wherever you go. They talk endlessly about runs past and dogs long dead, and know as much about pedigrees as any Newmarket bloodstock agent. All that passes above my head. I just go along for a bit of fun, the pleasure of watching good dogs at work and the entertainment of watching grown men and women too trying to drive three or four puzzled sheep in and out of four sets of hurdles in the middle of an empty field. A lot, too much perhaps, depends on just which sheep you are lucky, or unlucky, enough to get from the pen at the top of the field. I used to watch my old neighbour Llew Evans Blaensawdde, a champion in his day, train his dogs behind his house, and the hours and hours and hours he put into it persuaded me that if that's what it takes to get to the top I'd better resign myself to staying at the bottom.

Lambs were selling in August. I usually castrate the ram lambs, but because the weather was sultry I thought it wiser to leave most of them this year. I don't like to keep rams too long into the winter, as they play about instead of grazing quietly and growing fat. Before August was out I sold a big trailer-load at well over a pound a kilogram. Did I but know it I would have been better off, in fact very much better off, to have sold all my lambs in August and never to have gone near the mart on the day I bought the heifers. But then if I could predict the strength of sterling and the extent to which New Labour would be prepared to watch Welsh farming collapse I suppose I wouldn't be a sheep farmer but a currency speculator, or a politician.

> 'The Moving Finger writes; and, having writ,
> Moves on: nor all your Piety nor Wit
> Shall lure it back to cancel half a line,
> Nor all your Tears wash out a Word of it.'

Christine Evans

Friday, August 1st
Rather miserable day—drizzle and a sloppy sea, but *Highlander* brought three loads of day visitors, among them Meic and Ruth Stephens to see their daughters Heledd and Brengain, who are staying in Tŷ Capel.

Evening: get together at Linda's—25 of us—every household contributing a dish. Tim's pizza was spectacular. Cathryn had made fellafels. I took a sticky chocolate pudding and a dish of

SPICED VEGETABLE CRUMBLE
(Fills a 3 pint casserole dish; serves 6-12)
Fry 2 onions chopped finely in a little oil with 2 cloves garlic
Mix in up to 2lbs of whatever other vegetables are available—carrot, leek, beans, aubergines, parsnip, courgette, cauliflower, celery, peppers, tomatoes etc.
Add 1 tbs tomato puree
2 tsps curry powder
2 tsps chopped or minced ginger or ½ tsp fresh grated mixed to a paste
juice of a lemon
I pint vegetable stock

Simmer 25 minutes then place in casserole dish and add crumble (3 ozs flour, 3 ozs oats; 2 ozs marg rubbed in)
Sprinkle 2 tbs oil over top. Bake 25-30 mins in moderate oven .

We sit just inside Plas barn with the door open, and as the light fades, Linda lights candles that glitter in Niamh's specs (and mine, I suppose) and highlight laughing teeth. Outside, Mike is singing softly and playing the banjo; Tim has the squeezebox. Despite efforts to encourage him to be sociable, Iestyn is sleepy—his eighth party in his three-week life, Tim's said—and once when I am holding him he opens his eyes to the gigantic shadows dancing on the whitewashed ceiling, focusses wonderingly on the pattern of black beams and then, as if it's all too much to take in, heaves a huge sigh and closes them again.

Saturday 2nd August
Calm and dry—a busy changeover day. I cleaned Plas Bach and Carreg and then joined Linda in Tŷ Capel before dashing down to the Cafn to say goodbye to Annie Bates the wildlife film director and the rest of the dolphin-watchers. I'm sure they'll be back next summer. After lunch to the Observatory to hear about Esther's training course on Coll last week—the plans for her gap year teaching in Uganda seem very real now.

Sunday 3rd August
Rain all day. It started about 7.30, quietly gurgling from all corners of this solid stone house—a warm, whispering busyness outside each open window, trickling steadily into our tanks like the life-support fluid that we forget it is. Deep inside the fuchsia bushes by the back door the bees were still busy, and the tame robin and wrens and warblers on the wall seem to enjoy it. No point in my getting drenched (Ernest and Col. certainly will and drying clothes here is a problem) so I've retreated to the upstairs window to read Ted Hughes' *Tales from Ovid* and watch four boatloads of day trippers wandering about disconsolately under their waterproof hoods.

Monday 5th August
E—N.E. 5-6, gusting 7 or gale 8. Rainbow at breakfast time.
Strong easterly gusts. 2″ rain in an hour reported on the radio—
flooding in Devon and Cornwall and County Wexford.

A domestic day—baked three loaves, fruit cake and pizza.
Ann McGarry from the Centre for Alternative Technology came
down and we spent an hour enthusing about earth closets, solar
panels and windpower—I dragged her into our privy to explain
the way the waste would be scraped out into the holding bed
each week and sprinkled with lime; at the end of a year (before
ploughing) it would be spread on the fields. No problem—and
there was a 'gwas' to do it, probably a young lad to whom it
was no more unpleasant than carting muck from the farmyard
dungheap. Col. came in for tea and became keen on the idea of
building a wind-generator from scrap. In the winter we are to
go to Corris to see what can be useful over here.
Stonechat very loud on way up to the school, dancing about
above the gorse just beyond the mountain wall. Its song—*tsach-
tsach*—sounds exactly like hitting two stones together.

Saturday 9th August
S.W. 4-5 Fogbanks.
'A boiling sultry day' says Michael Fish on the radio—but here
thick fog, murk and drizzle. The Tomos family came for the
weekend—Dafydd Rhun excited about staying on with us.
Although he's only five, he's stayed with his Nain and he has
spent every summer holiday of his life on the island when his
dad was Trust Officer, so no worries about homesickness—only
will I have the energy to keep up with him?

Also on the Observatory boat Imogen Herrad from Berlin to
make a radio programme about the island for 'the German
equivalent of Radio 4'—she's come to it through literature and
obviously knows my book *Island of Dark Horses* in detail.

Sunday 10th August
Sunny and hot.
As a leaving present and memento for the Silcocks family, I've

121

planned a group photograph of all the summer residents on the same spot as the 1934 one on the wall in Dynogoch, so—seven men with two dogs, six women, five children and baby Iestyn assembled—by the old limekiln at eleven o'clock and Peter Hope snapped away.

Then a walk to the lighthouse and rockpools on Pen Diban —limpets and periwinkles, sea-anemones, starfish, shrimps and blennies flicking about in their salty gardens.

Monday 11th August
A sticky night of warm southerly winds and the day almost too hot and sunny as I sat in the garden being interviewed by Imogen. At half-past midnight Dafydd and I walked up to the South End to 'help' catch and ring shearwaters. Their season will soon be over: many of the adults have already left for S. America, the chicks following about three weeks later. Sarah pushed all three of her children snugly bedded down in the wheelbarrow; they looked angelic, blond heads in the moonlight.

Friday 15th August
Recording the weeds in our garden with Niamh, the Botany student from County Offaly. Cleavers or goose grass under the apple trees; the usual creeping buttercup, sow thistle, stinging nettle and small nettle, dandelion, silverweed and bramble. Among the peas and beans, the bright blue eyes of speedwell and scarlet pimpernel look so attractive I've left them—my excuse is, to conserve moisture—and in the potato patch, fumitory's purple flowers. Rare I think except in the west, but once a plant of power, its smoke (*fumus*) used in ancient exorcisms. No *papaver somniforum*—the showy opium poppy that comes up every year next door and in the North End gardens—but there's 'wart weed' (the sun spurge whose milky sap applied daily *does* cure warts), and hogweed with roots yellow and thick as parsnips. We've all developed a sensitivity to this plant, (an instant angry rash) so we treat both leaves and stems with respect. I dig out every piece with savage gusto. Its named in Latin for Hercules; my book says the plants are viable

for 80 years. Depressing reading: each dock plant can produce 50,000 seeds to be scattered or windborne or carried underground as nesting material by ants.

Sounds in the garden—bees, hoverflies, grasshoppers, wasps rasping, still stripping stems for nestbuilding.

Tonight the most vivid meteor shower since I was a girl in the dark fields above Scout Farm. I knew the earth was passing through the Perseids orbit as it does every August (the display so well known since ancient times it even has a common name, 'The Tears of St Lawrence') but was still startled, going out for a pee in the small hours, by the sudden silver flares and the glowing trails they left in their wake. I stood and watched them, in the mild-breathing summer dark, for over half an hour.

Wednesday 20th August
S.E. 5-6, increasing 7; heavy rain.
A big swell breaking grey and savage white in the bay. As we dressed, we watched the little dinghy *Ariane* (that was Col's before the Trust bought it) leaping and snatching on its moorings. But when we next looked out, it had pulled free and disappeared, and by the time we walked down to the point, there it was—sunk, awash in the breakers, being pounded towards the rocks. It is a terrible thing, quite beyond the logic of risk-assessment and insurance claims, to lose a boat on an island, and not known within living memory here. It goes against the instincts of self-reliance and survival, and to fishermen feels a crime of neglect of the craft they must trust their lives to daily, and care for almost as a farmer for his stock. So as soon as the tide had ebbed enough, Col and Tim scrambled out over the rocks and into the surf to get a line on the dinghy, load it with buoys and push it out afloat again. Then, despite the rough sea, they launched one of the fishing boats to tow it round to the Cafn, full of triumph and adrenalin—to be accused by the Trust manager of attempted theft and possible police charge! From the 'property' point of view, it seems impossible to explain that a boat can mean more than 'just a bit of wood and fibreglass'.

Of course, it was an exploit, and a matter of pride to them, but it had never occurred to the island men that saving the boat could be seen as *interfering*. Now as we sit listening to the gale, I realise it is we who are out of step, like the last families of the old nineteenth-century island community who, when they moved to the mainland in 1925 found it difficult to adjust to not working together, sharing food in times of plenty and of hardship, and healing their own differences.

Saturday 23rd August
6.30 a.m.—a strangely comforting thick grey mist, the foghorn lowing; suits our mood.

Goodbye to the Dawsons after a month; Mike's been coming every summer since his mother saw a newspaper report in the mid-fifties. Only 16 to the houses this week; the season already winding down. But a lively bunch of Young Ornithologists from Essex to the Observatory.

After supper, the rain cleared and there were a few streaks of red low in the west. We walked round the west, noticing the grass on Penrhyn Gogor rapidly becoming mattressy thatch since it's no longer grazed—the vegetation underneath has died.

Little Owl calling just outside as I write this.

Sunday 24th August
Dreamed of somebody finding a dead blackbird, and telling them how this year I have missed the taste of bilberries. Awake a long time before 5 a.m., when the dogs in the yard barked at first light—but when I got up found Dafydd Roberts had been in and left a bilberry pie on the kitchen table with a note from Esther about finding the fruit on Mynydd Hiraethog.

Ernest and Col. out round the pots at 7, then up to the lighthouse for a husbandry visit. A clear, dry morning, the garden full of bird activity—willow and greenish warblers, wrens churring, two young robins with adolescent speckly breast hopping close. A single swallow was swooping back and forth as if on wires. Bees busy in the fuchsias despite lack of sun.

Wednesday 27th August
Still galeforce, but slightly more westerly. Curtains flapping like trapped gulls, the sun a bleached apricot. As I walked up Pen Cristin, the gorse bushes squeaked and fidgetted in the wind. In the Cafn a ragged line of black gobbets of oil—and a second Trust dinghy washed ashore from the mooring and smashed.

Andrew from the Observatory took charge of gathering up and bagging the oil, which he thought could have been Sea Empress stuff disturbed from the seabed by the heavy swell. We left the dinghy where the tide had dropped it.

Col. baled the last of the hay after lunch—brilliant blue sky and scudding clouds.

Saturday 30th August
Calm all night: after so much wind-noise, the quiet kept me awake.

The young robin hatched in the small apple tree is still amazingly confiding. Today Tim reached out with one finger and stroked his breast feathers—the bird stayed on the fencepost until startled by some movement of the dog behind him.

Sunday 31st August
Planning a trip to the mainland—Col's hand is swollen, probably from an infected wrasse spine, and he's been feeling sick and feverish. There's a bad forecast, but we should be able to cross at low water. We are all glad this August is over.

ISLAND COMMUNITY

Which way you lean here
as in a boat, makes the rest
shift to stay afloat.

SEPTEMBER

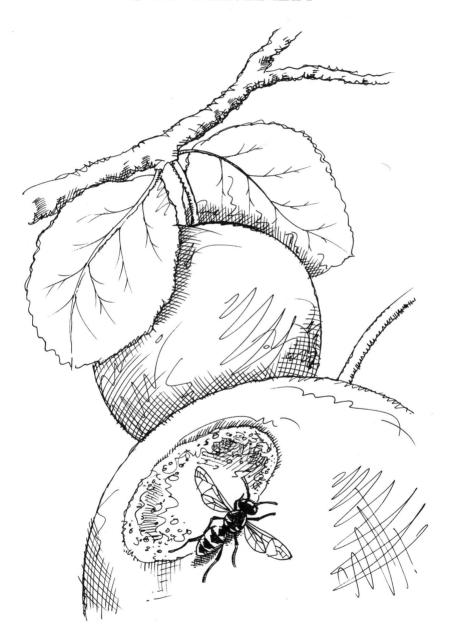

Wasps / *Picwn*

In his vivid depiction of the autumnal dying of 'The Wasp's Nest' the poet George Macbeth captures the pregnant moment when the 'bloat queen/Sick orange, with wings draped, and feelers trailing,/Like Helen combed her hair, posed on the ledge/Twenty feet above the traffic' and the poet realises that he could easily 'exterminate an unborn generation,' but that if she, the Queen survives, then 'all next summer' 'the stepped roof will swarm with a jam of striped fighters.'

I love that phrase, 'jam of striped fighters', to pretty much the same degree as I am wary of the wasps themselves, especially when September sees them turning their backs on a meat-eating summer and the alarm-coloured squadrons develop a taste for sweet things, hovering with invisible wing beats around litter bins, each drop of leftover pop a sugar refinery to the investigating insects.

My mam recently had a wasp's nest in her glasshouse in Pwll, Llanelli: a papier maché architecture that was both frail and resilient at one and the same time, a ghost balloon, a mummified football.

The wasps manufacture this extraordinary building material by chewing wood pulp, usually dry wood, rasped off with strong mandibles, and chewed until the mix of wood and wasp saliva turns into a mulch which then dries as a paste. The structure really is surprisingly strong, and contains the equivalent to a hatchery, a palace, palace kitchens, and extensive dormitories (with some reserved as royal apartments where next year's queens are reared), but I suppose anyone who has seen a long tailed tits' nest, built using tiny feathers found on the forest floor and employing no glue, cement or indeed no written plan other than some genetic blueprint handed on from adult bird to chick, shouldn't be surprised by such building skill. Look closely at the wasps' nest and you will see different coloured swirls and whorls, patterns which show where the wasps have chosen different wood to chew.

The so-called social wasps—although they can appear pretty antisocial to autumn picnickers as they home in on a cake or chocolate biscuit—are the black and yellow hooped ones. There are, in fact, more than 290 kinds of wasps in Britain but only a small proportion are true wasps or vespidae. How to recognise a true wasp from an impostor? The real counterfeit test is to check the wings, which fold into longitudinal creases when closed over the bodies of true wasps: the others lie flat on their backs, as it were.

True wasps include the commonest wasp of the lot, vespula vulgaris, which is the househunting type, often found to have built its small football nest out of papier mache in an attic or under the floorboards. Almost as common is the German wasp and both kinds are armed and dangerous. Of the seven species of true wasps one of the most interesting is the cuckoo wasp, which lives at the expense of a wasp called the Vespula rufa in whose nest the cuckoo wasp, as befits its name, lays its eggs. There is also that super wasp, the hornet, scarce in Wales though found in places such as the Wye valley.

The big conspicuous wasps that sometimes seem a sign of spring are usually young fertilised queens that have survived hibernation. A wasp colony is founded by just such a queen, who often chooses a site such as an old mouse-hole or cavity under the surface of the soil. The queen wasp lays a few eggs which hatch into grubs which are fed by the queen on a diet of dead insects until the grubs mature into worker wasps after a week or two. The workers then shoulder the burden of enlarging the nest and raising more young, leaving the fecund queen to the business of serious egg production.

By the late summer the wasp numbers in the nest have swollen to as many as two thousand, a beneficial number to any gardener because of the sheer numbers of caterpillars and other plant-destroying insects they carry back to the nest as snacks for the grubs. The workers collect the prey and in exchange the grubs produce a sweet substance for the workers—who love it much as they do ripe fruits, nectar and honeydew. When the queen stops laying in late summer and no more grubs are produced, there are no more sweet tasting secretions for the workers, which transforms them into buzzing nuisances, eager for their sweet-tasting fix, making do with jam and fruit, lollipop sticks and leftover lemonade which has them squeezing into discarded cans and—be warned—into cans left briefly unattended. Many a slip twixt cup and lip is what they say, but so too the occasional sting, as wasp and drinker are both caught unawares.

William Condry

When I got to the top of Cader Idris today I remembered that a mountaineer once told me a story which I've never known whether to believe or not. He said he was going up Cader from the south, groping through fog near the summit, when a noise behind him made him look round and there a few yards away was a non-human figure coming up the track. At first he thought it was a bear but when it came closer it turned out to be a monkey, quite a friendly one, and they finished the climb together. He claimed to have discovered later that the monkey was a pet belonging to a house down in the valley.

No doubt it was quite an adventure to meet with a monkey on Cader, even a tame one. A wild bear would have been even better but it is probably as long ago as the Dark Ages that bears were wild in Wales. The Welsh for bear is *arth* and you will find several bears on the map of Wales—Penarth, Llanarth, Aberarth, Arthog and I daresay others—suggesting that bears were once widespread. (But be warned that the etymology of place names is very dangerous country and that the apparent bearishness of these *arth* names may be totally misleading).

And there is Arthur himself, lying patiently under the stones of Craig y Dinas near Beddgelert (or wherever), awaiting the trumpet call that will bring him back to life. What did he have to do with bears? Could it be that in the imagination of our ancestors the retreat of the Celtic tribes led by Arthur, as the Saxon invaders advanced, became involved symbolically in people's minds with the decline of the bear, the defeat of Arthur coinciding with the extinction of the *arth*? Arthur may never reappear but will the bear be brought back one day? That looks unlikely as long as the Welsh uplands are so devoted to sheep.

* * *

I was sauntering, to use a word Thoreau was fond of, past a sallow bush three months ago when a tiny point of yellow-green caught my eye and when I looked closely at it I saw it was the shining egg of an eyed hawkmoth. It is nearly thirty years since I first learnt to recognise these eggs. 1969 was a quite wonderful year for eyed hawkmoth larvae hereabouts. In normal years I see very few if any. But in 1969 whole twigs of our local sallows were stripped of their leaves by these hungry caterpillars. Let me quote the *Country Diary* I wrote on September 6: 'With reckless disregard of birds, puncturing flies or any other enemies, they feed in full sunlight at the ends of quite exposed twigs. It is as if they had never read the textbooks which say that these larvae hide by day lying along the central vein of the underside of a leaf, their head towards the stalk, so that their transverse pale lines seem to continue the side-veins of the leaf and so achieve a marvellous camouflage. I began finding these caterpillars back in June but those early ones have long since pupated. Now it is September and still I see these splendidly huge, brilliantly green creatures that are so conspicuous against their dark-green leaves.'

From that day to this I have not seen another population explosion of eyed hawkmoths but I do recall a summer when poplar hawkmoths were swarming on the creeping willows in the sand dunes at Morfa Harlech. I do not know what normally keeps the numbers of these fine moths within strict limits. Some specific parasitic fly perhaps. What is clear is that at rare intervals the controlling influence fails to operate.

* * *

I have another vivid September moth memory. When an entomologist friend asked me for records of the goat moth I had to admit I had never seen one. But I did know just a little about its caterpillars and the strange attraction they have for red admiral butterflies. Years ago a birch tree grew close to our cottage in the wooded gorge of the Einion stream and one September day I was surprised to see about two dozen of these most beautiful butterflies clustered together on its trunk. When I looked round I could see others arriving through the trees, steering a wavering course against the wind but all homing in on this birch. Clearly what was attracting them was about a dozen small holes all close together in the bark about two feet from the ground. These holes were the work of larvae of the goat moth as they dug their way out of the inside of the tree where they had been living for several years, chewing patiently at solid wood. From the holes came an unpleasant stench and if you have ever smelt a billy goat you will understand how this moth got its name. What is surprising is that for several years after the caterpillars have gone their holes retain their odour and go on attracting red admirals.

It is strange how certain butterflies the world over have a love of the smell of putrefaction. In the south of England the purple emperor can sometimes be lured out of the tree tops by an offering of carrion. And in Kenya I once saw dazzling butterflies attracted by rotting bananas. At what stage in their evolution, I wonder, did these butterflies acquire a love of foul smells while the majority of butterflies find sweet-smelling flowers so irresistible?

* * *

September is the month for a very special flower of the mountains. The grass of Parnassus may come into bloom many weeks earlier in coastal dunes but today October is in sight and I have just been to pay my respects to the grass of Parnassus high on the crags of Snowdon. It is a grass only in the medieval meaning of the word—that is, any small wild plant. It is in fact a cousin of the saxifrages and was presumably named after the once holy Greek mountain as an acknowledgement of its special beauty, a flower fit for the gods. It can reach about a foot in height, its single erect stem topped by an exquisite five-petalled flower. Its Latin name, *Parnassia palustris*, suggests a plant of marshes and it was in a Snowdonian marsh that I first saw it in a September of long ago. It was growing (struggling would better describe it) in a jungle of sneezewort, devils-bit scabious and cross-leaved heath in a wet valley bottom under the spectacular crags of a corrie in the Carneddau—a suitably splendid setting for a plant named after such a distinguished mountain.

Patrick Dobbs

September started badly. As I was working on a wire fence above the road a large stone, more a rock really, rolled from the bank. It blocked the ditch. It looked like it shouldn't be there. Unprofessional. I decided to lift it out.

I knew it was a mistake straight away. I've done myself enough injuries to recognize some disasters before they happen, and this was one of them. But I went ahead just the same. I levered underneath the stone with strong posts, and tried to roll it up hill. Progress was slow, the job was taking too long. I grasped the thing with my hands, to lift it from the ground like a giant potato. I felt my back go as soon as I straightened up, the curious squelchy feeling of vertebrae sliding sideways and out of line with one another.

I wasted two days before I went to the osteopath. He is a magician, though he lives at the end of a long rough stone track which must shake up his patients as badly as it shakes up their motor-cars. I survived forty minutes of terrifying manipulation, and four days later I had recovered sufficiently from both injury and treatment to go sheepdog trialling. Solo won me a cup and a challenge trophy, and I was happy again.

The cattle trade began to slide in September. I got rid of three steers and two heifers in Sennybridge on the twelfth, not particularly well but well enough, but I took five heifers to Llandovery the following week and brought them all home again. I wanted more money. I thought I would do better next month. Store lambs were going all right, but buyers were choosy at the breeding ewe sales. Fortunately my older sheep had gone in the spring, just before lambing time, but I did try to sell thirty-nine ewe lambs on the twenty fourth. The price was disappointing, and I wouldn't part with them.

'The World is too much with us; late and soon,
Getting and spending, we lay waste our powers.'
William Wordsworth

Tregaron ram sale was a bad day again. Just as no Welsh town is quite like any other town in Wales, or anywhere else for that matter, so every livestock mart is individual and unique with a character all its own. Quite different from Tesco's or Marks and Spencer! If you want to sell well, get an early number and not be kept hanging around until after dark, you must leave Llanddeusant early. Six o'clock is none too soon, half past four is better still. Imagine, loading rams in the half light of a morning in late September! The wonder is I ever get there with the right sheep.

I took four to sell that day. Once arrived, and the formalities in the office completed, you look at the others as they come in. Some eighty per cent of them I reject out of hand. Too big. Too small. Too young. Too old. Too thin. Too fat. Too soft and usually when it comes to it too expensive. I want a very particular kind of ram. He must be tough enough to survive being turned out on a strange mountain with several hundred ewes. He must have a good fleece to keep out the rain and tidy, regular teeth that won't drop out the first time he chews at a bit of sugar beet. He must have good feet that won't let him down in the high rocks or on wet fields. And he must, of course, be likely to transmit all these virtues to his offspring.

One thing he must be is a real mountain ram. If there's a hint of a black sheep in his family, ears like a donkey instead of a mouse, of a fleece that says cross-bred all over he won't suit me. He should come from a good place where he's used to the mountain air. If I don't like the vendor I won't buy his sheep.

As it happened I didn't buy any sheep. I sold three of the four I took, far too cheaply, but I might as well have kept them for I'll have to go to another sale to get the rams I need. What do you do in Tregaron mart when you've seen all the sheep, exhausted the possibilities of original conversation, had all the tea you can afford and it will be three hours before your own sheep get their sixty seconds in the sale ring? Bird watching? Not a happy day. Next month I'll try Aberystwyth.

It's the eighteenth of September and I must drop in to the school to vote for a Welsh Assembly. I remember last time, when Edward Heath swore it would lead to the break-up of the United Kingdom. I didn't believe him, but the very idea of it made me campaign all the harder for the Labour government that promised to deliver. But Labour in power changed its mind, as they so often do, and people in Wales agreed with them. Now it's been William Hague's turn to threaten us with the break-up of the United Kingdom. Our Assembly's coming, but the British state with all its warships and guns and arrogance and the extraordinary House of Windsor and its obsession with a World role that is a hundred years out of date seems as immune to disintegration as a clapped-out nuclear power station. Why anyone should be expected to serve, love or respect an institution without equality, justice, generosity or compassion is beyond my understanding.

> 'Ah Love! could you and I with Him conspire
> To grasp this sorry scheme of Things entire,
> Would not we shatter it to bits — and then
> Re-mould it nearer to the Heart's Desire!'

Land drainage is what I really have on my mind. Some years ago I had plastic pipes laid under stone chippings in some of my wettest fields, and now at last a contractor has come to finish the job by dragging a mole plough above and across them so the excess rainfall flows quickly away. What a welcome sight! I don't know that I quite agree with the East Anglian farmer who said that water flowing from a drain is absolutely the most satisfying thing in the whole world, but it certainly had me jumping up and down with delight in the bottom of the ditch.

The end of September was the end of my four geese. The grass is on the turn, and a corn-fed goose is a very different dish to a green one from the fields. I killed them in the early morning, before anyone might be about, with a blow to the back of the head. Not a nice job, but as any hangman or machine- gunner will tell you, once you've done the first it gets easier as you go along.

Christine Evans

Wednesday 3rd September
Heavy rain, more dismal than yesterday. Halfway to Caernarfon for Ernest's 9.30 optician appointment, we were behind a car which skidded and hit a beer lorry lumbering up round a bend on the top of Yr Eifl. No one was hurt, but the elderly woman in the car began to have chest pains. We sat with her while the rain lashed down and wind rocked the car. It seemed a long time before the ambulance arrived, and another country entirely from the bright sun of last week.

Friday 5th September
S.E. 4-5, occasionally 6.
Set off back to the island just after midday through a big, stomach-churning swell and whitecaps, wondering how the tensions would have resolved. It's such a small place, emotions get exaggerated, personalities magnified or drained, as Brenda Chamberlain described in *Tide Race*. And it matters to us

particularly because it seems that we belong to the island—not just a place of work for a few months or even a few years.

A year ago this week I saw the first sick rabbit in the hayfields, and a few weeks after that, the vast families that thronged the banks and scurried in the bracken had all gone. Though I've walked all round, early and late, with binoculars, there's been no sign of any survivors; four outbreaks of myxomatosis never succeeded in such a decimation so perhaps it was the new virus R.H.D. Carried by birds or insects, perhaps? There's no sign of it in Uwchmynydd, where rabbits are still common, even in neighbours' gardens.

In 1291 an inventory of Bardsey noted the value of rabbits and skins in the same breath as that of cattle and sheep. I don't expect the island has been without them since, and until our more finicky times they were a most valuable food source. The Trust will need to re-think its grazing strategy, for with the big reduction in stock numbers and keeping the mountain free of sheep for five months of the year, the choughs already seem to prefer the close-cropped slopes just across the Sound—I counted sixteen on Mynydd Mawr this week.

Sunday 7th September
The lovely quiet of September mornings—no gulls or seabirds shrieking about territory, just the warblers' busyness, robin, wren and blackbird—a deep breathing peace seems to have settled over the island in this spell before the great waves of migrants start.

Sat watching fulmars performing their slow air-dance and by my left hand were tiny spiders dangling on invisible threads flung across the grass.

Warm, windless evening. After supper we walked down the west as far as Solfach where we met Llew and Dick by the hide—they're over here on building repairs, but first came with teachers from Pwllheli Grammar school when the Observatory was set up forty years ago. While they reminisced with Ernest by the lighthouse, I stood in the dark and watched the great wings of light moving over smooth black water to the pale sand and round again. The sea was almost silent.

Tuesday 9th September
N.W. 3 veering S.W. and increasing later.
Pink sky this morning. Pleased to see a white wagtail on the yard wall; then Paul, the assistant warden, told me there'd been forty of them around Cristin.

Sitting at the wooden table in Tŷ Pella kitchen, listening to the baby's little sighs and moans as he works himself up from sleep towards the next feed. There's also the slow tick of Tim's clock behind me—calm and measured, as authoritative as if it came from an ancestral long-case instead of a plastic teapot freebie from Tetley's. Now and again, the demijohn of pink rhubarb wine burps decisively. Through the window, the rain-dull sea is smooth to the horizon.

Tim's gone fishing early so Dot's milking the goats. She called over the wall and I came in with my scribblings, making space for my notebook among the the remains of breakfast—a half-pound of butter, the heel of a homebaked wholemeal loaf, the brown teapot in a woollen cosy with its bobble drunkenly askew. I've settled into the chair, knowing the chapel pew along the back wall is handsome but too narrow for comfort. Overhead are slung the last two pieces of home-cured bacon and a few lumpy smoked sausages and there's a yeasty warmth, not really a smell but a ghost of yesterday's baking of loaves for the lighthouse painters, and perhaps the three barrels of homebrew under the window and the fermenting wine contribute to it. I think of Alice Thomas-Ellis calling happiness a 'by-product' that can't be deliberately sought or earned, realising that in this calm moment, precious because it will be broken any second, I am in possession of it.

Friday 12th September
N.W. 5 or 6.
Windy—good drying weather. Flocks of swallows on migration —over 300 counted yesterday. Col. busy with the binder, harvesting barley and oats. A late spike of Autumn Ladies' Tresses on the bank is a curl of small white flowers the nearest thing to green. As if they have been drawn upward, as clay is

turned on a potter's wheel, and spray is shaved off a breaking wave.

Tim picked hops from behind Nant to dry for brewing in the winter—a great heap of soft infolded cones with a fresh sweet smell. They give the bitter flavour to beer and help it to keep longer.

Thursday 18th September
N.E. 5 or 6 later.
Moonlit silver and pearl all night. I dreamed of being one of a fisher community living far out in the warm shallows of an inland sea or a vast lake, on rafts tied together behind nets, a summer floating suddenly threatened by the men returning shouting from their small boats news of a tsunami, a great Surge that was coming . . . Woke at 5, with the first breath of wind, and lay wide-eyed in this solid stone house three fields from the sea, but with the sense-world of the dream fading only slowly—the gentle rocking and warm breath of the clear green water.

Col. was up before 6. I heard him striking a match to light the candle downstairs. Then he was out to get lambs in, load them and launch the Sea Truck. By 7.30, wind was starting to whine in the kitchen chimney and though Tim and I took another trailerload down, there was a huge swell breaking on the Gaswellt, brilliant as ice in the sun, and as the Seatruck swept in, Ernest waving both arms across in a No-Go gesture. Very photogenic but I never have the camera at the right time.

Spotted Flycatcher in the apple tree.

Monday 22nd September
S.E. 4. Fair. Good.
Tim and Dot are away this week so I am enjoying the farmyard round—milking and taking the goats out, feeding the kids, the dogs and poultry, and walking round the sheep. Dislike filling the haynets, though: my eyes smart and big itchy lumps spring up on my arms. Willy the billygoat is docile enough, too friendly in fact—I take it as a mark of affection that he tries to

140

pee on me. There are worse smells than concentrated ammonia, I suppose . . .

Gannets diving on the west—soundless spurts of white drew my gaze. Blackberry picking, met up with Bob and Lis Normand who pointed out a Great Northern Diver in very smart summer plumage, black head and white speckled back, swimming around as though the little sandy bay were a lake in the icy wilderness.

The month of Daddy-long-legs at dusk, legs trailing incompetently. A woodmouse dragging a broad bean over the backdoor step—just waiting for us to leave?

Sunday 28th September
S 3, later 4 or 5.
Stooking corn sheaves in the sun. Swarms of goldcrests in the garden—legs no thicker than wire. Andrew and Paul ringed more than a hundred caught in the mist nets this morning.

Tim and Dot back from the mainland; I have to confess to having put the hens off lay and having mislaid some bantam chicks.

HAREBELLS ON THE MOUNTAIN

So delicate they
tremble in the breeze's play,
summer's parting breath.

OCTOBER

Bramble/*Mwyar Duon*

The bramble or blackberry is one of the plants that almost everyone would recognise, especially by taste. There are four hundred microspecies of bramble in Britain and there are unique bramble communities in Wales, although you need to be a bit of an obsessive expert to tell them apart. But in the mouth they are simply the taste of autumn.

The berries, blackberries, are a tart-maker's delight, that is as long as they're picked before the 10th October. It is an old belief that the devil cursed the fruit when he was cast out of Heaven on the first Michaelmas day and fell into a bramble bush. In the late eighteenth century, when whooping cough was a social scourge, it was common to pass children through a bramble bush and immediately afterwards to make an offering of bread and butter, left at the base of the briar. The belief was that the disease was left behind with the food.

That wise old herbalist Culpeper assessed the bramble thus: 'the berries of the flowers are a powerful remedy against the poison of the most venemous serpents: as well drank as outwardly applied, helpeth the sores of the fundament and the pile.' Similarly, blackberry vinegar was by many people favoured for the treatment of colds and coughs.

It is, indeed, a hugely beneficial plant for people and for birds and animals. The thick underground rootstock sends up innumerable thick stems which have a veritable armoury of defence mechanisms—from prickles to hooks and hairs. The stems grow to such a length that they arch over and when the tip touches the soil it will eventually take root. In this way the bush thickens over a plot of earth, turning a patch of ground to impenetrable tangle, a miniature thorn forest. Being a deciduous plant it loses its leaves in winter to become a desiccated cascade of brown stems. In the summer, bramble flowers are a larder for butterflies and bees, and wasps also make, well, a beeline to feed here, their round gossamer wings all ashimmer as they picnic among the petals. The plant will flower well into the autumn with some new flowers appearing as late as October, although these won't bear fruit. But when the fruit appear, especially if the bush isn't systematically denuded by basket-carrying platoons from the local Womens' Institute, it will attract wasps aplenty, many small insects, determined birds adept at defeating the defence systems and maybe a late fox or perhaps a hedgehog on a last feeding frenzy, eager to store enough fat for the hibernating months. Oh, and flies, such as the ones in Sylvia Plath's poem 'Blackberrying' which turn a bush of ripe berries into a bush of flies 'hanging their bluegreen bellies and their wing panes in a Chinese screen/The honey feast of the berries has stunned them; they believe in heaven.'

Birds, in experiments, express a strong preference for red, black and to some extent blue fruits—the colours of ripe berries rather than the yellows and greens of unripe ones. Seventeen species of bird have been recorded eating autumn blackberries, especially in September and October, with blackbirds being the commonest, although ring ousels, song thrushes, starlings, bullfinches, greenfinches, blue tits, great tits, whitethroats and their less showy relatives the lesser whitethroats, have all been known to invite themselves to the feast. There are two peaks of activity; one early in September and the second from late October into early November. The first comprises mainly blackbirds, robins and warblers eating blackberries in bushy places such as thickets or wood edges. The second wave is made up almost entirely of gregarious and noisy starlings which, having finished the elderberry crop, turn to the blackberries growing in field hedges and along roadsides.

Man and blackberries go way back—back as far, in fact, as the Neolithic age. Seeds have been found in the bodies of one of those crazily preserved people cocooned in clay near Walton-on-the-Naze in Essex. Although nowadays the fruit is the only important part of the plant for man, the spine-covered skin was formerly stripped and peeled to leave a pliable rod used for thatching and tying brooms. Close examination of the fruit will reveal that each berry is made up to 15-20 drupelets, each with a single stone, a complication of miniberries making up a juicy architecture.

One Welshman was very important in the spread of the bramble. Hywel Dda, who created a series of laws in the 11th century, declared a system known as *gavelkind* which divided land equally between a man's sons rather than the old way known as primogeniture, which handed on the land to the eldest son. Dividing the fields led to smaller fields and more hedgerows which sped the bramble's journey through the land.

A bramble bush, ripely purple, is a part of everybody's childhood memory-tapestry; indelible smears of delight around plump mouths; carrying milk bottles or baskets of squishy fruit. They were never gathered, though, without some drawing of blood, without crashing through a spiny jungle. Blackberrying is a quest.

William Condry

When I parked my car opposite the village chapel today I was pleased to see that even now, on the first of October, there was still a flower or two bravely showing on that delicate-looking but in fact strongly elbowing plant, ivy-leaved toadflax. It was blooming, I remembered, back in May, and had been decorating that high wall ever since. When its flowers are getting over it turns them round to face the wall in the hope that they will drop their seeds into crevices where they will germinate instead of being dropped to the ground and be wasted, for this is a plant that does best on walls. It is not a native species but has been insinuating itself enthusiastically into the British wild since at least 1640. Before that it had been grown in gardens, brought here from Italy perhaps.

An undated flower-book on my shelves (I guess it to be mid-nineteenth-century) is enlightening about the spread of ivy-leaved toadflax in west Wales. It quotes a man who wrote to a magazine reporting it growing on a rock near Barmouth. He wondered if it could be native there. This brought a response from another man who wrote: 'I here declare that several years ago, in one of my numerous tours through that and other mountainous regions, I carried a box of seeds of this beautiful and tenacious plant, which I distributed in appropriate places on rocks, ruins, churches, castles and bridges, where I have since beheld it thriving in tresses and festoons to my fullest satisfaction. I particularly remember sowing it on the rock he mentions.'

The book goes on to point out that not every botanist approved of such introducing of aliens but then comes down firmly on the side of the introducers, commending everyone 'to become disseminators of new beauties over our native land, for the benefit and gratification of future generations.' It was in this spirit that the Alpine Garden Society sowed (with very little long-term success) many alien species on a cliff on Snowdon in the 1930s. Such a venture would be more strongly disapproved of by most naturalists today than it was years ago. They remind us of the devastating effects of the spread of the rabbit, the prickly pear, the Colorado beetle and countless other scourges the world over.

* * *

The other day I took a train at Tywyn on the coast of Cardigan Bay and let the Talyllyn narrow-gauge railway convey me gently inland to Abergynolwyn station. From there I headed north, following a zigzag trail that climbed through an oakwood to give me a lovely view back to the high ridge of Tarren Hendre, two miles south. Soon the wood degenerated into closely planted spruces which cut me off from all panoramas. Above the belt of spruces I reached open ground whose views were all to the north across the green valley of the Dysynni. I walked down into a world of pastures and scattered birches and before me rose Craig yr Aderyn, its slopes crossed by the long-tumbled walls of an Iron-age fort, its crown a rugged outline against the sky. I sat awhile on the summit rocks enjoying the sunshine and watching a family of choughs playing and calling musically in the breeze off the sea. I thought of what

Lewis wrote in 1840 in his *Topographical Dictionary of Wales:* 'Craig y Deryn, or the Rock of Birds, derives its name from the number of birds which shelter in its crevices during the night.' Strangely there is no mention of the unique inland breeding cormorants which Edward Lhuyd had made famous long before. What birds had Lewis in mind, I wondered, that roosted so numerously in those fissures? Cormorants do not roost in fissures but could the birds have been choughs? Certainly scores of choughs roost there these days, autumn and winter, hiding in the many cavities. There could well have been more back in Lewis's day, for choughs are thought to have been commoner then than now. I would have tarried much longer on Craig yr Aderyn enjoying the cheerful company of the choughs and, after they had gone, the aerobatics of buzzards and ravens doing gymnastics in different parts of the sky. But I had a train to catch.

* * *

For many years one of my favourite works to browse through in the National Library at Aberystwyth has been those many volumes of newspaper clippings called *Bye-Gones.* They cover a wide range of topics, chiefly local history with a generous scattering of natural history, mainly in north Wales and the nearby English counties. They begin in 1871 and go on well into the twentieth century. Particularly fascinating in the early volumes are the sometimes detailed accounts of the field frolics of local natural history societies. We read of the long miles they went in wagonettes, on horseback or simply on foot. Some of those clubs have faded away long since. There was the Offa Club, for example, and the Oswestry and Welshpool Naturalists' Field Club. But others are notable for their longer duration: I think of the Woolhope in Herefordshire and of the Caradoc and Severn Valley Field Club in Shropshire. A century ago the members of these societies enjoyed a countryside which in many ways was more blessed with wildlife than is today's countryside. I am thinking of the herb-rich meadows, the bird-rich marshes and the many oakwoods now gone.

I would have enjoyed being on the six-day meeting organised by the Caradoc and Severn Valley in June, 1904, and 'attended by twenty-two ladies and gentlemen.' They went by train from Shrewsbury to places like Corwen, Trawsfynydd and Bala, then transferred to horse-drawn carriages or set off on foot. Some walked the moors to a lake where 'thousands of black-headed gulls rose into the air, screaming and whirling about like huge snowflakes.' They got caught by rain 'but they were not daunted by it though six of the party were ladies.' At Palé, near Corwen, a well-known naturalist, Thomas Ruddy, showed them his fine collection of fossils. At Lake Vyrnwy they did well for plants (wood geranium, globe-flower, butterwort and starry saxifrage) but would have missed the ring ouzel if a very good bird man, H. E. Forrest, had not pointed it out to them.

I am especially remembering these venerable societies just now because I was recently at a party to celebrate the Montgomeryshire Field Society which for fifty years has held its AGM, elected its officers, arranged its programme of meetings (which have an outstandingly good attendance record) and produced its annual report telling us what has been going on in the world of nature and conservation. When I wrote an account of this half-centenary in the *Guardian*'s 'Country Diary', I mentioned the long duration of another local society, the Powysland Club, founded in 1867 and which I described as the oldest archaeological society in Britain. I might have guessed what would happen next: I very soon got a letter from a lady in north-west England, pointing out that their local club is in fact one year older than the Powysland.

A propos of absolutely nothing I can't resist passing on this gem which caught my eye among the *Bye-Gones* of 1903. It recalls an interesting record from back in 1754: 'On September 30 at Ewe-Withington near Hereford was married Robert Phillips, Esq. to Miss Anne Bowdler. Mr Phillips is upwards of 80 years of age and the lady very little less . . . This courtship is said not to have been less than 60 years in agitation, which has been postponed in courtesy to some relations who disapproved the match.'

Aberystwyth is a lovely town. Sea, interesting shops with books and fresh fish and cafes and hippies and happy students and a ram sale where I could do business. I was bid twice the money for my two year old than I was offered in Tregaron, although I still took him home. I bought a couple of Welsh yearlings of my type, as well as a big Suffolk to go with the older ewes. Although it is a long way from Llanddeusant there was no need to leave before dawn, the whole sale only took a couple of hours and there were enough suitable sheep to choose from. And it was held on one of those magical autumn days when the promises of spring are all fulfilled and the toils of summer seem all worthwhile.

The following week I took ten heifers that had done their work on the overgrown pastures down to Sennybridge mart and only sold two of them. [Taking heifers to a local mart, getting a derisory bid for them and taking them home again was, did I but know it, to become almost a way of life over the next few months.]

When worry and the stresses of life threaten to get the better of me I find the best way through it isn't mental turmoil but physical effort, and in my job I can call it work. There's a corner of the paddock across the road where the peat has filled a giant hollow in the impervious clay. I saw a large tractor disappear there once, and lost a cow in it years ago. I've fenced it off since, and made it secure to some extent by planting alders and willows, but the peat still oozes down and blocks the plastic drains I laid deep in the field beyond. So I got a shovel and dug I should think six feet down, and I found water and then I found the drain. I collected a small trailer load of three inch chippings and put them round the pipe, then put little stones on top, and bigger stones on top of them until I had a sort of giant soakaway by the field fence. It seems to work, the ground beyond is firm and dry and the once waterlogged soil is fertile and productive.

Several of the woodland paths leading up to the mountain have become blocked with thorns and overhung with branches of hazel and birch. To ride along them, even to walk, is hazardous. Is there anything nastier than being scraped by a blackthorn? So I took the chainsaw and spent a few days clearing the ways and clearing the mess afterwards. It's the sort of job that tends to be put off day to day, week to week and year on year, but it improves my everyday working environment so much I wonder why I didn't do it ages ago. How nice to be able to attend to little things, like a wet patch in a field or an overgrown path!

On the morning of the twentieth of October I sold thirty-three ram lambs in Sennybridge and that afternoon I sorted out a hundred and thirty-four ewe lambs to go down to Salisbury plain for the winter. They were all dosed against liver fluke and the one or two lame ones had their feet trimmed and sprayed with a suitable antibiotic. Their ear and pitch marks were checked and put right where necessary.

I was out on the mountain every day that week, on the old bay cob with the young mare Gwenda doing an evening shift. As well as sheep you seem to come across a hiker or two over every rise and down every dingle nowadays. I like seeing children and families paddling in the river or playing in the rocks—just so long as they don't climb my boundary fence! Most of them keep out of the way and wait for stock on the road, but sometimes they're a real nuisance, with dogs chasing about just when I want to bring the sheep down. I have even disturbed a party using a spirit stove to boil their kettle on a bale of hay in my barn. Although many graziers see them as completely alien, a lot of them are in fact local people and speak Welsh.

'. . . the hills are diminished.
They are a gallon of petrol,
There and back . . .'

Herbert Williams, 'The Old Tongue'

All the sheep came in eventually, as they always do. This year they're in good condition after the wet summer. The odd few thinner ones, any yearlings changing their teeth which makes grazing the mountain pasture difficult, and younger sheep which I just don't fancy the look of I put by to run in the fields with the Cheviot rams. The older ewes, to be sold as breeding sheep in the spring, go to the Suffolks to throw the bigger black-faced lambs that lowland farmers look for. The bulk of the flock stay with the Hardy Welsh, for they alone can survive and thrive on the system that suits my particular farm and way of farming. We were fascinated with the breeding and domestication of animals before Xenophon wrote his treatise on horsemanship or Hannibal marched his elephants over the Alps, and the problem is to combine fitness to survive the rigours of life with the capacity to produce as much milk, muscle or work as possible.

The rams went to the ewes on the twenty-seventh of October, so the first lambs will be due on the twenty-sixth of March next year. The main flock with the mountain rams are penned in a field overnight so they mix and get to know one another. The following morning they are driven straight up to their walk on the mountain. The older ewes with the Suffolks have a goodish field, and the rams have blue raddle on their chest so I can keep an eye on what's going on. The Cheviots in another field are raddled red, to tell me which is which. Let's hope the winter will be kind to them, and they all produce a lively lamb in five months time!

Christine Evans

Wednesday 1st October
A thick grey start to the day; couldn't see beyond the garden wall at 7 o'clock but as I watched Ernest walk down the track after breakfast, the mist cleared in front of him—when he

reached the Narrows, suddenly the lighthouse was there, sunlit, waiting, and soon after the foghorn ceased its insistent blare. Then the sea noise was evident, and the crash of the swell breaking on the west coast rocks. I did a load of washing, spreading the sheets over the gorse bushes by the old Limekiln as previous generations used to. The bracken on the mountain is a rich red quilt now, and the patterns of the small fields gone under it are beginning to show through.

Blackberry picking in the middle fields and behind Nant Withy, it was obvious the island belongs to the birds again—no human noise to be heard, and thrushes and wrens hopping about as though they have forgotten already that they have to share the world with us. Choughs still enthusing, and a couple of curlew calling wistfully.

The sun lingered, very red, pillowed on cloud; then a brilliant blue sky darkening to show off its first two stars. In the garden, the apple tree began letting go of its leaves one at a time, very gently.

Thursday 2nd October
A day that floats Ted Hughes' line 'October is marigold' to the surface of the mind. It is, and crossing the Sound in shirt-sleeves, bright blue, and silver too—metallic colours, exhilarating. All the sweeter because it must be shortlived. A Red Admiral making the most of the sun on the bedroom windowsill in Cae Hen where the garden is a jungle and alive with small birds resentful of our grass-cutting. Despite the swallows lined up on the telegraph wires and the robin's autumn song there was a sense both of feasting and secret germination.

Saturday 4th October
S.W. becoming S. and increasing 5-7, perhaps locally gale 8.
Calm morning waking slowly out of cloud.

Writing on the mountain today (calm and overcast, pleasant but not as unseasonably warm as yesterday). Up Pen Cristin past the big white rock, Col's childhood 'Ty Gwyn', lichen furring every fissure and spike, and on up over the crest, Peg sniffed each gorse bush hopeful of rabbits. I tried it too, and was surprised how unpleasantly musty the gorse smells now, not coconut. There were sheep turds neatly laid out and as inoffensive as a little girl's plaits and several shells of huge puffballs, Bakelite brown; I thought the first was wind-scattered plastic until I touched it with a foot and it disintegrated in an exhalation of thick brown dust. There's still a sprinkling of heather flowers and each dead foxglove spike is held firm by its green rosette of eight leaves. From the top the island's topography is a pattern of greens (brightest where the springs rise), greys and browns—two fields of stooked grain, the lines not quite straight despite our efforts. Ernest is lifting lobsterpots far off on the west, and Tim and Col. are working a line of tide in the bay for pollack or late mackerel.

I am ghosted all the way down by a group of curious ewes.

Friday 10th October
N.W. 5-6.
Dry, bright, blowy and cold waiting in the Cafn for the Highlander, which had to turn back on Pen Cilan. So we all went carrying oats—the lighter stooks bowling along in the wind. I drove the David Brown slowly along the rows. The gang of builders who hadn't been able to go home for the weekend came to help, and then all to Plas for a cup of tea.

Saturday 11th October
N.W. becoming cyclonic for a time then N. 6-7, possibly gale 8.
11.30: Just back from meeting the Pwllheli boats in the Cafn, fingers stiff with cold so it's not easy to write. The wind dropped in the night to leave this morning quiet that always amazes: a solitary curlew calling over the fields to where the sea lies as smooth as the water shining in the tractor ruts. When we left the house just after 8.30 the sky was heavily overcast and it was starting to rain, but there was no wind at all. The tractor had to be bump-started down the slip, there were problems loading, and the wind began to freshen as the tide turned; a lot of physical effort in unpleasant conditions. Not a place for the

weak or old—or women, indeed, unless they are a lot stronger and more competent than me.

Sunday 12th October
N.W. then N. 6-7.
Lighthouse cleaning. Cold and bright, all the island colours sharp, the bracken like a ragged shawl pulled close on the mountain's shoulders. I sat in the hide right on the tip of Pen Diban and watched flocks of birds streaming over the south end of the island—some flying back and calling or landing to feed a bit more as if they'd realised this is the last service station before Pembrokeshire.

Monday 13th October
N.N.W. 5-6, occasionally 7.
Garden digging. Scarlet pimpernel, buttercup, hogweed all growing vigorously. The cold snap and the wind direction are bringing waves of migrants in, notably the first big flocks of thrushes. More than 300 redwings drawn south by the migrating sun, even more goldcrests—what a season it has been for them, though watching Andy and Paul fat-scoring and ringing them, it's obvious these last broods are in much poorer condition and few will survive. How prodigal nature is with these small lives.

NORTHERLY

Winter's ice-bright breath
Pushes the pale sun southward
Redwings in its wake.

Wednesday 15th October
Wet and windy.
Walk with dog before bed north through the hayfields, the sky alight with an unseen moon, I was astonished at the amount of growth, clover and long grass, since the summer. Several low-flying jets passed overhead and on the way back I saw orange lights popping out like fireworks off Pen Cristin—like *Lord of the*

Flies—a 'message from the world of the grown-ups'. The world of targets and new weapons tested from Aberporth.

This place feels like a real world, not just a retreat *from*. And certainly not just a jolly holiday trip. Susan Cowdy's rallying cry, when the Trust was first set up in the 70s: 'We must stop Bardsey becoming *a holiday island* . . .' It's a life of few time-fillers: no driving, shopping, telephone chats or television; for me, a series of small challenges—managing the temperamental oven so the bread doesn't burn, getting the conditions just right so that the yogurt 'yogs' satisfactorily, making sure the drinking water buckets are full before the rain stirs up the well, keeping lamp wicks trimmed, the privy sweet. Domestic satisfactions, physical exertions, deep animal content.

I like living surrounded by sea, by the breathing presence of the sea and aware of the perpetual movement of the sky—cloudshapes, swirls of weather systems fretting the winds and shaping the waves, the migrating flocks following the sun as the earth turns. I feel caught up, part of a huge growing process.

Saturday 19th October
Variable 2 or 3.
Rosy dawn about 7.45 now (study of the tide book shows the days are shortening by two minutes morning and evening.) Col, Ernest and Tim crossed in the Sea Truck to get the post and stores and to fetch the new, expensive rams and the winter feed-blocks. They were back by lunchtime, as the last of the Trust visitors left, and then went turning oat sheaves in the bottom field.

This may be the last mild day—it was warm even on the mountain, and a strangely still evening. Saturn low in the east as the sun set, then Venus very bright over Ireland.

Monday 21st October
N.E. 5-6, squally showers.
Dot's Open University exam, by special arrangement taken at home with the Island Warden invigilating so I was Iestyn-sitting. If he'd needed feeding she could have had a break, but I

managed to tire him out so he slept until just before the three hours was up. Ernest and Col. (busy clearing out the old engine room at the Lighthouse) spotted a seal pup in one of the coves near Bae Nansi.

Wednesday 23rd October
E.5. Fair, good.
Bitingly cold but dry. Finished the digging and tidying in the garden and made apple chutney. This week I've also scraped all the paintwork in the kitchen ready for next spring.

Drove the sheep in this afternoon—the last time this year—two ewes doubled back on the back of the mountain. The rams, all being feasted on the aftermath in the hayfields, are getting increasingly impatient.

After supper I walk down to the field where Col. is tending a fire of old bales and prunings—a glowing red-gold mesh, flowing like lava, showers of stars as he pokes sullen stuff into flame. It's the time of year for fires—pagan celebration and childhood excitement. We dance about, chase each other and the dog through the smoke and then become almost hypnotised looking into the heart of the fire, savage heat on the front of the body, biting cold wind on the back. Tim comes down, and Linda, and a couple from Cristin, and they make enormous, gesticulating silhouettes against the red as I shiver back to my den in the dark.

Friday 31st October
Leaving the island, the air was almost ominously still, the sea calm as grey glass or just-setting jelly.

NOVEMBER

Barn Owl/*Tylluan Wen*

Thankfully, there has only been one occasion when I had the soul scared out of my skin. It was a day of dismal mist, a cloying cottonwoolness of the stuff over everything, all the reticulated creeks and runnels of the marshes of north Gower near Llanrhidian dangerously hidden. All the signs so necessary for fixing a bearing in a salt-marsh were smothered by acres of dense fog and I was stumbling blindly towards Whitford with its iron lighthouse, navigating the dissected marsh, with cleverly treacherous areas designed for sucking off a wellington boot and leaving one with a cold muddy foot to contend with on top of everything else.

I was hugging the fenceline which controls the wild ponies when, with a white rush of wings, a barn owl came up out a creek where it had been feeding. My heart fibrillated and jolted and I could understand why these birds have for so long been associated with ghosts and spirits, the bane of anyone rash enough to fall asleep in a churchyard where these birds are hunting. It disappeared with gentle wing beats, a white presence receding into the grey mist. Of course the barn owl isn't all white, but the clear white breast and the disorientation of the event made it seem so, a large white moth trailing a grey cloak of fog. One Welsh name for the barn owl is *aderyn corff*, the corpse bird. A Gaelic name is poetry in itself—*Cailleach-oidche Gheal*—the white old woman of the night. Wordsworth, in his poem 'The Waggoner' panicked at the sight of one:

> Yon owl!—pray God that all will be well!
> Tis worse than any funeral bell;
> As sure as I've got the gift for sight
> We shall be meeting ghosts tonight!

In her book *Folklore and Stories from Wales*, published in the first decade of this century, Mary Trevelyan noted that 'the flight of an owl across a person's path was very baleful.' But some writers have gone even further. Count de Buffon maintained that 'if it perches upon a house and utters cries a little different from ordinary, it then summons inhabitants to the tomb.' A less fanciful way of seeing things is that those engaged in the dreadful job of watching over the dying, and sentries on less stressful duty would, of course, be more likely to hear owl shrieks rend the night air.

The bird has even given its name to a part of the day, owl-light, the cusp between night and day, or gloaming.

One of the Welsh language's finest poets, and a more than competent ornithologist to boot, Dafydd ap Gwilym, wrote in the 14th century a poem which examined the owl's pedigree. The owl, talking in verse to the poet, tells its story, how it was once a chief's daughter but was changed into an owl by Gwydion the magician. Shakespeare, more prosaically, said, 'They say the owl was the baker's daughter.'

As food becomes scarcer and the days draw in so one's chances of encountering a daytime hunting barn owl improve. This Gower bird was abroad in mid afternoon, unexpected and, when my nerves had settled again, a remembered delight.

With a body covered in small feathers which smother the sound of its approach, the owl is a hunter par excellence. One ear is set slightly higher on the head than the other, which means the bird can home in with pin-point, or perhaps talon-point accuracy, on its prey—even in complete and utter darkness. It adjusts its head so that the tiny sounds of, say, a mouse walking towards its fate, are the same in each ear and then its face is aligned perfectly with the direction of its prey. Its disc-like face also helps it collect sounds from the night—and sometimes the day—toward the ear. Its eyesight is acute: the barn owl is able to detect objects with a surface brilliance a hundredth of what man can see. It can use its call to communicate with other owls, usually to mark out territory but it sometimes uses its screeching call to frighten small mammals into breaking cover. The bird may fly silently, but its call, a prolonged and strangled shriek, is the sort of sound to still a field vole's heart.

Sadly the barn owl has declined in numbers in Wales as old barns become entirely derelict or conversely get turned into bunkhouse accommodation. Rough grass, a prime habitat for small animals, is much scarcer than it used to be and its eyes, which are slow to adjust to changes of light, make the barn owl very vulnerable to the dangerous and often lethal mixture of plentiful food on roadside verges and fast cars.

Long gone are the days when owls nested in human habitations in great number. The Rev M. A. Mathew in his *Birds of Pembrokeshire* of 1894 noted an 'owlery' which was located in 'some old cottages, just below a beautiful Henry VII church tower. The roofs of the cottages all communicated, and were tenanted by such a number of barn owls that at last the cottagers rose up against them, being annoyed by the smell and the noises proceeding from the birds, and we were informed that between forty and fifty were either driven out or destroyed.'

The poet and naturalist John Clare loved the barn owl, a fact as transparent in his verse as a barn owl is beautiful:

> Now the owl on wheaten wing
> And white hood scowling o'er his eyes,
> Jerking with a sudden spring,
> Through three-cornered barn-hole flies.

'A wheaten wing.' Perfect, Mr Clare.

William Condry

By making a garden at the edge of an oakwood we inevitably created a Shangrila for wood mice which rejoiced in the cover of our new shrubs and in the delicious rowan, cotoneaster, pyracantha, berberis and other berries on offer. At first we fought against the invaders, live-trapping them and exporting them far afield. But they were all quickly replaced, so great is their passion for reproduction. We soon gave up the unequal struggle and when we discovered that crocus and tulip bulbs are strawberries and cream for wood mice we resigned ourselves to having a crocusless, tulipless garden and learned to accept, even to admire, our mice. They are, after all, truly beautiful with their shiny, brown backs neatly divided from silver-white underparts, and with their prominent ears and large, lustrous eyes. They seem ever taut and nervous and exploding with life. Catch one alive and the likelihood is that he will give your finger a nip, spring triumphantly out of your hand and go bounding away with athletic leaps. Adventurous and enterprising, he will squeeze into your house through amazingly small apertures. And that's where the real trouble starts because he not only plays the house mouse to perfection but is even more destructive, being larger and stronger. He will eat almost anything. He climbs like a squirrel and just as outdoors he will nibble at the cordon apples up your wall, so indoors he will scale your library shelves and make nests of your books and papers.

So to live at peace with wood mice you must keep them out of the house at all times though you tolerate them in the garden. There, even though their numbers are 'as autumn leaves that strow the brooks in Vallombrosa' (I love that line from Milton), yet you will very rarely see one except by torchlight because they are so nocturnal. To enjoy their company you need to go and sleep under the trees without a tent some warm summer night. Then you will hear them rustling and pattering all about you and even find them taking short cuts over your sleeping bag. I well recall the nearest I ever got to really close terms with a wood mouse. I had drifted into sleep as I lay on the floor of a wood and was slowly brought back to consciousness by the realisation that a mouse was gnawing very, very gently at one of my finger-nails. I wonder what he thought of it?

* * *

If ever I had to choose my favourite ancient monument, I'm sure it would have to be that astonishing bank of earth which

164

was built for all those miles down the border between England and Wales in the eighth century. 'Here,' decreed King Offa, 'is England; over there, where the sun sets, is Wales.' Not his precise words, I daresay, but his intention was clear enough; and the two countries have kept much of their separateness ever since.

If some ancient monuments, for all their wealth of history or pageantry, leave me unmoved, that is no doubt something lacking in me, not them. But Offa's Dyke never fails to appeal. I like my ancient monuments to be simple and direct, far from towns, preferably away over the hills or out along the sea cliffs, places where buzzards and ravens sail and circle and larks and pipits sing. I think of Maen y Bardd, a Neolithic dolmen which has looked across the Snowdonian landscape near the Conwy estuary for something like four thousand years. I remember my delight at first seeing that perfect memorial the Bronze Age left on Bryn Cader Faner, high on the north end of Rhinog—a circle of outward-leaning stones so evocative and photogenic out there on that lonely moorland. Or I think of the next age which gave us all those hill-crowning forts that preceded the Roman time and were still in use, a few of them, even when the Romans left centuries later. Good places to walk up to, these hill-forts, to sit awhile and contemplate life and time and evolution, while a healthy upland wind blows through your thoughts.

A few centuries after the hill-forts along comes the English Offa who left his mark on history in many ways but nowhere more firmly than by this high bank and deep ditch (no doubt then far higher and deeper than they are today). I like to think of the stone castles that have come and gone while Offa's work has remained. I also enjoy the happy way the Dyke has often turned up in my life when I haven't been thinking of it. Perhaps I am botanising in Montgomeryshire or birdwatching in Radnorshire. I choose a high, inviting bank to eat my lunch and enjoy the view. Only then do I notice that this bank stretches away far to the north and south and that yet again I have landed on Offa's Dyke. It is like meeting an old friend.

Inevitably after twelve hundred years the Dyke is far better preserved in some places than in others. You will often see where trackways and roads have been cut through it; but these are pinpricks compared with the wholesale sweeping away of the Dyke across some of the farmlands. We can be thankful that much of it belongs to the uplands where it has been preserved by remoteness and the absence of the plough. Up there you can still find long stretches where it breasts the slopes and curves round the contours in great beauty. Offa's laws and other acts are long buried in the archives while his earthy bank endures from age to age. What king has a finer memorial than this much-cherished Dyke?

Patrick Dobbs

The Welsh rams with the mountain flock tend to form monogamous relationships, and as I want every ewe to have a lamb I go up on the bay cob Firs to chase them around so they have different partners. A solitary ewe might entice a couple of rams down Nantmelyn dingle or out on Pantygwin's walk, but if I push them back to Fan Foel there's a good chance they will make new friends. In recent years fewer graziers turn their ewes back to the mountain once they've put the rams in, and my sheep wander further afield looking for the freshest pasture. A score or so often settles above Afon Llechau and there may not be a ram with them, so the dogs sweep round them and send them scuttling back to their usual haunts.

Frazzles the chestnut mare has lately developed the dangerous habit of lashing out at the dogs if they brush past her heels. Bobi has already been kicked and keeps well clear, but young Tobi comes with us now and he trots along practically underneath her. I hate to see animals hurt, and especially if I feel responsible for their injury, so I settle for safety and trundle sedately along on the old bay gelding.

He gets a helping of oats first thing every morning, and another when he comes in from work. Slowly, almost imperceptibly, he loses the fat of summer and the muscles on his neck and quarters bulge and harden. There can be few more satisfying ways of spending two or three hours of a bright November day than shepherding on a fit horse with a team of enthusiastic collies.

The ground sheep, running in two bunches with the Suffolk and Cheviot rams, are brought in to the pens every two or three days. The ewes with a fresh raddle mark over the tail are counted and pitch-marked blue or red on the shoulder so they won't get counted twice. If they're in good condition with sound teeth and feet they join the mountain flock to reduce the number competing for the limited grazing in my tiny fields. The rams need another dollop of raddle, powder paint mixed with oil into a treacly porridge, to be rubbed into the short wool between their forelegs.

All the half-bred lambs are sold, so I keep the crossing rams for year after year until the infirmities of age make them incapable of further service. There's a Cheviot here who must be ten or twelve. His front teeth have all fallen out, but he manages well enough with his gums, and his lambs are still as plentiful as they are unmistakable. Each season I think must be his last, but he's been around so long the place won't be the same once he's gone.

Big rams, fit and fat, are very heavy. Turning them over, so they sit on their backside nestling between your knees, is quite a knack. I put my right hand under his chin, my left in front of his hind leg, and swing him over using my knees as a pivot. No chance is as good as the first chance, and like most weightlifting jobs, if you get it wrong you're in trouble. When he rears up on his hind legs he's as tall as I am, and I feel his breath warm on my cheek. The old Cheviot isn't a lot smaller than the Suffolks, and though he's lost the agility of youth he's artful with age.

I swing him up and thump him down, and when I've put the raddle from chest to belly and he walks away I see I've done him a considerable injury. His hind leg is dragging. He is unsteady. He lies down. Old bones are brittle, and I wonder whether I have dislocated his hip or cracked his pelvis. I feel sick. One thing is certain, he's not going to serve any more ewes for a week or two.

He was injured on the fourth of November, and I kept the old fellow until the twenty-fifth by which time he was walking well enough. I doubt if he has any bones broken, but he has no future. Although I may never find as good a one again I take him down to Llandovery mart. I get twenty pounds for him, and he'll be dead by dinner time tomorrow.

'And fear not lest Existence closing your
    Account, and mine, should know the like no more;
The Eternal Saki from that Bowl has pour'd
    Millions of Bubbles like us, and will pour.'

On the seventh I get a telephone call half expected on a Friday night in November. Phil Fish will be round with his hounds tomorrow. I'm not well pleased. Years ago my heart would quicken to the sound of a hunting horn and the cry of the foxhounds. They brought colour and excitement to the fields and woods, but now it has turned more sour. This is a shooting pack, where the foxes are bolted from their underground sanctuary with terriers and driven into the open with hounds, where they are shot as soon as they are seen. The followers claim not to do it for sport, but they all look pretty jolly to me. They kill a lot of foxes, but the overall population stays fairly constant and there are as many now as there were thirty and forty years ago, despite guns, hounds and wires. The foxhounds disturb the sheep and destroy the tranquillity of the countryside, and I know that some of the most enthusiastic followers, who seem to think they can go where they please with their guns and motors, are most vociferous in their hostility towards people who want to walk along paths or on the mountain. I could just tell them to keep off, but Phil is a nice enough fellow and most of my neighbours make him welcome.

'The fox drew in and flared his muzzle.
Death was there if he messed the puzzle.
There were men without and hounds within,
A crying that stiffened the hair on skin,
Teeth in cover and death without,
Both deaths coming, and no way out.'

John Masefield, 'Reynard the Fox'

In November my ewe lambs leave Pantyscallog on their long trip in a big lorry to Salisbury plain. They share the journey with ewes from Everitt Brynglas, and it's a bit of a squeeze to get them all on. They look too tight to me, but the lorry driver is very experienced in livestock haulage, and should know how many it's wise to carry. I take two Suffolk rams and seventy-eight ewes to finish off the grazing, and reckon that when my seasonal tenancy expires at the end of the year it will have been well worth the price I paid for it.

Christine Evans

Saturday 1st November
St Cadfan's day.

R.S. says April is a month for listening; by the same logic, November must be the month for smells. Autumn on the mainland is more smoky—the air smells of the ashes of old camp-fires, fungus and fermentation in the woods. The earth is still warm, seeds feeding from the husks as they shrivel.

The stone's not back yet on the grave of Ernest's parents. It's hardly healed since Nellie's funeral nearly twelve months ago, a jumble of lumpy clay.

> To your still-bare grave
> I bring first and last heather
> from Mynydd Enlli.

Tuesday 4th November
S.E. 5-7, locally gale 8; continuous heavy rain.
A day for indoors. 8lbs green tomato chutney and 6 of apple jelly.

Ernest and Col. to Southend to investigate a landing craft as replacement for the Sea Truck which apart from being old (and originally bodged up from a wreck) is too small to carry diggers and heavy tractors across the Sound. They left about 6, and were back some time after midnight after horrendous hold-ups near Milton Keynes. A fruitless journey. Made them appreciate where we are lucky enough to live.

Peg only got a a ten-minute walk, just up to the old Army camp above our fields, where I stood looking at the loom of the lighthouse across two miles of misty sea, thinking 'Here I am again'—despite the comforts of the Rayburn, hot water and a warm bed, it feels akin to exile.

Friday 7th November
S. then cyclonic 3-4.
Calm and dry. Col. back on the island—Ernest scooted him and the post across when the wind dropped yesterday afternoon. After shopping in Pwllheli (bare trees in Nanhoron reminded me this is a year I've seen none of their leaf-change and fall) I got back to winter digging and clearing. I stuck a few clippings of the Euonymus in a vase on the kitchen windowsill to enjoy the reddish seedpods against glossy green leaves. I lit a bonfire of hedge trimmings and garden rubbish before the pile could be colonised by creatures—the hedgehogs ought to be safely tucked up, but shrews stay active—in the coldest weather, they can apparently slow their metabolism right down by *shrinking* their internal organs—and wrens are always on the lookout for winter shelter. Last year, when I reached down to drag out the old bluetit box from where it had fallen behind the windbreak, there was an eruption of six or seven of them, a whole family stuffed inside.

A noisiness of ravens in the back field drew me to investigate. They'd found part of a lamb carcass and pulled it out of the hedge where it probably crept to die back in the summer.

Saturday 8th November
The Bardsey Bird and Field Observatory Council meeting in The Ship in Aberdaron. I walked through the bracken dying so splendidly on the headland (choughs and ravens) and along the clean, deserted beach. In the pub the atmosphere was business-like, all those people beckoned outdoors by their passion for nature grimly huddled over bits of paper. Good to see so old friends like Bill Condry and say an official farewell to Andrew, who's been a caring and diplomatic Island Warden. I shall miss him and his family.

Thursday 13th November
Sunny, mild. Calm enough for Col. to bring the mini-digger off Enlli in the Sea Truck and take back all the winter supplies of fuel and feed. Each calm day now is a bonus, a chance to stock up and shore up against winter. It can't be the same on the mainland, unless you live in one of the few places left inaccessible by road, like Scout Farm where I was brought up in the Pennines, or where Clyde Holmes lives high above Bala; vehicle-less, phoneless, even if not light-less, we need to be much more in tune with our old instincts.

Rounding a bend on the way to Abersoch this evening my headlights caught on a flutter of white—a barn owl swooping over a young fox, with a rabbit sitting by the side of the road—frozen in fear, I assume. Fox disappeared over the hedge and I drove slowly past the rabbit, but on the way home there was a corpse—probably the same one—run over. Perhaps it had already been sickening with myxy.

Before bed the dog leads me up the hill and over Wil Gwyddel's re-seeding, the wet grass sparkling. The pasture is still lush—it was quick with rabbits in the moonlight. (They love these little old enclosed fields with plenty of cover.) I sit on a stone to enjoy the serenity of the big ice-bright clouds. On the way down past the pond, the bushes rustle with roosting thrushes and redwings I saw earlier.

Saturday 15th November
S.W. 5-7, increasing later.
Mild and misty (15 degrees). Trinity House phoned late last night to say they'd lost contact with the Lighthouse, so we went up to Mynydd Mawr first thing. There were a couple of hares and thirteen skylarks passed overhead. Choughs very active, and eight ravens posturing like butchers round some woolly bits of sheep being unpicked in the bracken and spread over the apron of land where the old church was.

Big gale forecast—the lunchtime TV chart showed 40 knots for tomorrow—so Ernest and Steven got the lobster boxes in to take up to Holyhead before the weather breaks.

Hoping to see some shooting stars from the Leonids shower (comet Tempel-Tuttle) but it will be too overcast. Blowing hard now.

Monday 17th November
S.W. gale 8 to severe gale 9 and locally storm 10.
Wind still violent, strong enough to lean back on. The helicopter to the lighthouse took only 25 minutes from Swansea, doing about 200 knots.

Saturday 22nd November
Thunder and lightning in the night, but a 'weather window' so Ernest crossed at low water with post and to check the lighthouse. Home with Col. about 4 (already going dark).The Trust year is really over now—Linda came off too, having finished 'winterising' all the visitor houses and there's no one left there now but the Tŷ Pella family—Tim, Dot and Iestyn.

Wednesday 26th November
After two days in schools—yesterday poetry-writing with year 7 in Ysgol Glan-y-Môr, today readings in Menai Bridge—I find my appreciation of quiet and fresh air sharpened. On Mynydd Mawr the gorse bushes squeaking and fidgeting in the night wind, I savour the fresh smell of air from the west, like line-dried washing, and the amazing variety of fungus. Parasol and

horse mushrooms and tiny brown and sulphur yellow things called, I think, 'Hare's Ears'. Puffballs the size of a decent orange, their skin soft as kid gloves or horses' muzzles, the flesh smooth and sliceable as good bread. They taste and smell like field mushrooms only stronger, but they don't keep—decomposing suddenly into horror-film gunge—and they're not to our taste.

I love to walk through the half hour when 'light thickens'— as it gets dark starlings make wing to the withies round Pwll Ciw, and the Little Owl starts calling. To walk through darkfall, movement slowed as if in water, is to feel part of the night, and to come in out of it gives a sense of power. The kitchen brims with warmth and white light, the richness of the casserole bubbling in the Rayburn and the smell of airing linen: it's both welcoming and constricting. With flushed cheeks, the breath controlled and deep, pupils large as a cat's and ears tuned to small movements, for a moment you are between worlds and reluctant to shrink back into routine.

Sunday 30th November
In the harbour in Pwllheli where I parked to shop, a scattering of dunlin and golden plover, and one shabby cormorant mooching about.

Kim (just back from three weeks in India with Artists for Nature) walked over this afternoon, and described elephant-riding and watching the tigress Sita and her half-grown cubs so vividly I could feel my brain whirring away processing it. Eager now to see her sketches and paintings. She has a tight schedule, lots to do before February—and as is often the way what she feels like doing is a series of prints about *this* landscape, hares, bare fields and the winter sea.

DECEMBER

Holly/*Celyn*

We may associate holly with Christmas but its use in ritual goes back to pre-Christian times, probably associated with the feast of Saturnalia, named after Saturnus, who, reputedly introduced agriculture to Italy then called Saturnalia, or the land of plenty. It was a custom among the Romans to send a bough of holly to friends, along with other gifts. Pliny the naturalist, who lost his life in Pompeii, admitted planting a holly bush outside his house as a defence against witchcraft.

Before the nineteenth century, timber from holly trees was much sought after, with pollarding practised from the Middle ages onwards. Holly wood has a hard, fine, white-grained texture, resulting from its slow growth. It has been used instead of boxwood for making blocks as well as engraving.

One can rely on Culpeper to assemble a fulsome list of the virtues of such a plant. 'The berries expel wind, and therefore are profitable in the cholic. The berries have a strong faculty with them; for if you eat a dozen of them in the morning fasting, when they are ripe and not dried, they purge the body of gross and clammy phlegm, but if you dry the berries and beat them into powder, they bind the body, stop fluxes and bloody fluxes.' A timely warning here, though, because holly can be poisonous to man if ingested in large amounts. One painful medicinal application for holly was its use in recent centuries to deal with chilblains; people would use sprigs of holly to beat the chilblains in the belief that this would improve their circulation.

One species of butterfly takes its name from the holly tree: the holly blue butterfly which uses it as a food plant.

Birds love it equally and seven species have been recorded as being particularly fond of gorging on the berries—mistle thrushes, blackbirds, wood pigeons, collared doves, redwings, fieldfares and song thrushes. They may work methodically, starting at the top of the tree and working downwards and, with trees seemingly varying their weeks-for-ripening, one tree may be stripped of its fruit while a neighbouring tree is left untouched—for a while! Holly berries make a remarkable larder for birds, because the berries are long lasting, they do not go bad, they do not drop to the ground, and are resistant to extreme cold.

The behaviour of mistle thrushes around holly trees is fascinating. One bird, or sometimes pairs, will defend a holly tree against the attentions of other birds, thus conserving a long-term supply of berries to last through the winter, but when food is really scarce the defending thrushes may be overwhelmed by hungry intruders. Only a few trees in any given area are coveted and protected with such zeal.

Very few seeds can germinate immediately on leaving the parent plant, most needing a resting period first. Some species take very little time: willows and elms, for example, can germinate in a week, but holly takes a long time, up to twenty months.

Holly is the only evergreen tree found regularly in hedgerows and although it may reach a height of forty or fifty feet it is usually not much more than a tall bush. The famous seventeenth-century diarist John Evelyn had a champion holly hedge, the sort you could really brag about:

'Is there under heaven a more glorious and refreshing object of the kind, than an impregnable hedge of around four hundred feet in length, nine feet high, and five in diameter, which I can show in my now ruined garden at Say's Court (thanks to the Czar of Muscovy) at any time of year, glittering with its armed and varnished leaves? It mocks the rudest attempts of weather, beasts and hedge-breakers . . .'

Armed leaves it may have but not all of the leaves on the holly are prickly; the fierce leaves are found lower down on the tree where it is likely to be attacked by browsing animals—such leaves normally have twelve to fifteen sharp spines. Above some eight to ten feet above the ground these may be absent. The leaves in olden days were used as winter feed for sheep and cattle.

There is no doubting that holly is a tough plant, a born survivor. It can tolerate regular cutting and should a fire kill the tree above the ground it can still regenerate afterwards. It is more tolerant than most trees of frost and drought—with many adaptations to help it cope with adverse conditions. The waxy surfaces of the thick leaves, for instance, enable it to resist water loss when the soil is frozen. In summer drought young plants may shed their leaves and replace them the following year.

Like several other trees, holly was believed to be the tree from which Christ's cross was fashioned. The tree is alive with symbolism—the spines represent the crown of thorns, the white flowers the purity and the birth of Christ, the red berries drops of blood and the bitter bark the passion.

The old name for holly is 'holm', a component of many place names such as Holmsdale, Holmbury and Holmswood. It was grown in special woods in medieval times giving rise to Hollings as a place name. It also gives rise to the occasional poem. Hilary Llewellyn-Williams knows about holly and in an eponymous poem she notes the holly saplings under graveyard yews 'like prongs of resurrection,' and notes its 'deathless leaves.' Deathless: a tree of resurrection, a red flourish in the heart of a winter wood.

William Condry

Lately I've been thinking of badgers, probably because I've seen more than usual dead along the roads. Sad to see so many but at least they indicate that badgers on the whole are still in good numbers here, surviving among the farms and villages as they have since man first invaded their world far back in prehistory. Perhaps in the beginning badgers lived out of doors in broad daylight like deer or wild cattle but were driven by man's hostility into leading such a strictly nocturnal existence that we hardly ever see one except occasionally in the lights of a car.

That was how I saw one last night. I turned off the main road into the lane to my house and there going ahead of me was a badger, speed 8 m.p.h. For a hundred years, before it turned off into a gateway, I was able to see how heavily, almost awkwardly, it ran, hastening as if reluctantly because unused to such exertions. The shambling gait of a bear came to my mind; and it was as a bear that Linnaeus classified the badger. Today science places the badger firmly among the weasels but he certainly lacks the weasel's lissomness and quick movements.

Is it not rather wonderful that so large an animal as the badger has managed to survive so long in Britain and now follow the bear, the wolf and the beaver to extinction at the hands of man? The extent of its underground workings must be part of the answer. Some of these setts are centuries old, very profound and labyrinthine, with many exits and roomy enough not only for badgers but also for foxes, stoats, polecats, rats and rabbits. Years ago I heard of an even less likely occupant of a badgers' sett—a sheep dog that was fascinated by a badger colony which lived quite close to a farmyard. Whenever he was off-duty this dog would slink off to the sett, using it as his kennel. His master had only to whistle from the farmyard and the dog would appear, do his work among the sheep and then go back to the sett. For several months the dog occupied part of the sett while the badgers used other entrances. I would love to relate how the dog eventually gave up farming altogether and threw in his lot with the badgers. But this is not a story from Aesop or the *Mabinogion*—and the sad truth is that eventually the dog came home one day with his cheeks bloody from what was thought to have been underground combat. Whatever had happened he lost all interest in the badger sett from that day forth.

* * *

December's weather was, as usual, full of variety. On the showery first day I was at Llanbedr on the Meirionnydd coast, walking along the causeway across the salt-marshes to Mochras, seeing redshanks, curlews, teal and mallard. What I was chiefly hoping for were hen harriers, for this is one of their regular winter spots, and I was lucky. I was looking at a stonechat on top of a gorse bush when into the field of my binoculars came a male harrier, then a female, floating across the marsh with the perfect bouyancy that harriers achieve so well. For several minutes I watched them as they wandered away over the sand dunes, always hunting, seldom seeming to catch anything. Yet they live.

Showers and sunshine played with each other for days. On the fifth the wind switched from west to east bringing long hours of brightness and also a new bird for our garden list—a male merlin which perched on the tip of our tallest balsam poplar, his blue back gleaming in the sunlight. The weather went on dry and brilliant with frost at night, perfect for picking out the colours of redpolls, siskins and goldfinches acrobatically taking seeds from alder cones just outside our garden. On the eighth, at the western end of Talyllyn Lake, in the brightest sunlight, I stood amazed as if by a mirage. Looking east up the lake towards the pass, I could not see the lake itself although I was on its bank. All I could see, looking into the water, was a staggeringly vivid and flawless reflection of the colourful Cader Idris scenery perfectly imaged because of the absolute stillness of the water.

By next morning the anticyclone had gone and we suffered days of deepest gloom. But it cleared at last and on the 17th I went south for my annual pre-Christmas sea-cliff walk, this time on New Quay Head. The wind blew cold off the land as I followed the coastal path to Craig yr Adar. Time after time fulmars went circling out over the sea to swing back to the cliffs as if longing to land but never quite achieving it. Apart from herring gulls they were the only seabirds: the razorbills, guillemots and kittiwakes of this coast belong to spring and summer only. By December 21 a howling gale had set in from the east, nights turned very frosty and despite days of total sunshine it was an ordeal to go out of doors. Then quite unexpectedly Christmas Day was calm and delightful. But south-east Europe was reporting the century's lowest temperatures and the year ended with us looking anxiously out at flurries of snow, hoping they did not presage blizzards.

December, and forty-six ram and wether lambs are still unsold, beside a load of Llandovery heifers. The beef trade is bad and BSE some kind of excuse for it, but the sheep trade is worse and small lambs unsaleable. Oriel Jones, the Llanybydder butcher, usually takes my little mountain lambs for export to Barcelona, Milan or Portugal, but the strong pound and cheap sheep from Poland and Slovakia have done for us. What shall I do with forty-six lambs nobody wants?

If it doesn't pay to feed them it can't pay to starve them, so for the first time in my lifetime never mind theirs they get a bit of dried grass and sugar beet pulp. Most soon learn to change their eating habits, and scrum heads down at the trough like a pack of forwards at the old Arms Park. One or two are stand-offish, and they must make do as best they can on winter grass and bits of bark and moss and anything else they can scavenge. There doesn't seem to be much future for hill sheep, or hill farmers either come to that. We will have to change our ways, that at least is certain.

Friday the thirteenth and it's bad news. One of my ewe lambs died in the lorry on her way to Salisbury plain. The driver swore they weren't loaded too tight, but I thought they were and complained to my diary about it.

The weather is playing all sorts of tricks. One day snow, then fine and sunny then as wet and windy as it gets. I've decided to refurbish the sheep pens. I built them in 1969 when the old communal dipping bath on the edge of the common, which at one time everyone used but no one maintained, became so ramshackle that you spent more time stopping sheep climbing the walls than poking them into the dip.

For many years, of course, dipping was compulsory, and you could assess the thoroughness with which the job was done by the number of dead trout in the river. Eventually aldrin and dieldrin were banned, and we had to use organophosphates which killed fewer fish but left most of us complaining of something that felt like 'flu but a good deal more sinister. More recent alternatives have been better for people but much more dangerous to wildlife, and the old soakaway that I dug nearly thirty years ago has become unsatisfactory and illegal. In fact there are so many streams and all the fields are so steep on the Blaenau it's virtually impossible to dispose of used sheep-dip without hiring a contractor to pump it from the bath and take in away in a tanker. The old bath leaked as well.

I attacked the old pens with crowbars and a sledgehammer, and though they had gone to look a bit tatty there was no way they were going gentle into that good night. The oak gateposts, four feet down and rammed round with rocks, were worn and rotting by the hinges, but deep in the ground they were still as hard as the timbers of a tea clipper. The wooden gates fell to pieces quite easily, and I plan to replace them with weldmesh on a galvanised frame. The railings should be off-cuts of larch, but as all the local foresters seem to be felling Norway spruce this winter it is very hard to find.

Now for the dipping bath itself. First I replaced the rotting covers with slabs of seasoned oak, two inches thick, that I bought years ago to make into a kitchen table. The wood was so tough even the chainsaw found it hard going. It seemed a pity to use it for sheep, so I had another idea. I tipped large rocks into the bottom of the swimbath, then threw stones on top, finally blinded it with gravel and sealed it over with four inches of concrete. From now on injections and sprays will have to do the job of keeping the flies and ticks, keds, mites and lice on the run. Who says we don't move with the times! To finish it off I planted ten little conker trees alongside the collecting pen, so I can measure the years that remain to me in the spread of their shadow.

Christmas, and the holiday brings a plague of sightseers and hikers. They leave their motors everywhere, and one afternoon I cannot get on to the mountain because someone's blocked the gate by the grid. If they parked an old refrigerator or a grand piano by the roadside they'd be prosecuted, but they feel free to leave their vehicles just wherever they wish. And fifteen years ago you'd stop whatever you were doing and take a look at any strange car going by in winter!

My son Jason came home for Christmas week and we took a goose from the freezer and cooked him up, and he really was something special. Jason brought a carrier bag full of Christmas goodies with him from Luxembourg, and they're a lot better then the Chinese rice whisky he came along with last year. I can eat and drink most things, but not rice whisky! I wonder where he will be this time next year. When I first realised that Jason, fiddling with computers in a bank, was making as much money in a month as I earn in a year I found it hard to adjust. But now he makes as much in twelve months as I will earn in my life, and all I can be is happy for him.

On the final Sunday in December my daughter Briony came over from Switzerland. We roasted a sirloin off my best bullock, and drank red wine and ate curious alpine biscuits that tasted of cinnamon with icing all over the top. Before the year was over she too had flown back to her computers and the mountains that make Wales look flat with a few little hillocks.

I've been raising sheep, cattle, horses and all sorts of creatures all my life, but children are the real lottery and if I live for a thousand years I will never fathom how I came to rear them. In the meantime the dogs need their supper, and the cattle could do with another bale of hay.

'Yon rising Moon that looks for us again—
How oft hereafter will she wax and wane,
How oft hereafter rising look for us
Through this same Garden—and for one in vain!'

Wednesday 3rd December
S.E.2-3.
Fog and frost over whole of Britain.

Yesterday, an angry sky at first light, snow flurries as I drove into Pwllheli for a day's work in school but clear by afternoon, though freezing. Today's the first real day of winter —minus 1, all the trees and hedges dusted with glitter. The sky was red as lava before cooling to a delicate lavender blue.

Col. took a day off the drystonewalling to cross to the island with Ernest. They arrived on Enlli with the post just in time to help Tim get the old cow back on her feet—sometime in the night she must have slipped and gone down in the mud round the bale-feeder. It could have been something of a crisis with nobody else to help—one reason why the cattle are better left out in a sheltered spot is the possibility of an accident in the barn (they have magnificent spreading horns these Welsh Blacks) when Tim's on his own.

On Mynydd Gwyddel in the dark, the grass is so short and soft it is like walking on fur.

Sunday 7th December
S. 6-7.
The barometer 'dropping like a stone' Ernest said last night and we woke to rain driven against the window by a southerly gale. A day for Christmas cake-baking and being distracted from letter-writing by watching coal tits feeding (sunflower seeds). Quite a few birds come regularly now. The robin appears as soon as I put out his favourite sultanas and grated cheddar. There's no singing—no territorial defence.

However many nets of peanuts I put up they are always busy, with a queue of tits in the escallonia, chaffinches and sparrows waiting hopefully on the ground underneath. and blackbirds skulking about to see who they can mug. The berries on the sea buckthorn attract other birds, sometimes even a blackcap.

Selwyn phones from Melbourne—it's 40 degrees there, too hot to sleep. 'Full moon here, huge, but of course we see it upside down—you can't see the man in the moon in the southern hemisphere, the Chinese say it's a jade rabbit . . .' Half my mind is ten thousand miles away, but what I'm looking at is the sky grey with storm, the trees lashing frantically, the wind howling.

About teatime the rain eased off and by the time the half-moon rose, the wind had gone round to the west.

Wednesday 10th December
Shopping and a visit to the Archifdy in Caernarfon (researching the building of Bardsey lighthouse and its effect on the island community). The moon was clear on my left as I drove home down the long peninsula, and Jupiter and Venus bright and beckoning ahead.

As a symbol of 'good will' and sociability, robins are misplaced on Christmas cards—there was a tremendous fight outside the kitchen window this morning. Reminded me of Gwyneth Lewis's lines

Nid tincial tiwn ond bygwth trais
mae cân gylfinir a dryw'r helyg

(Not pretty tunes but threats of violence/ are the songs of curlew and willow warbler).

Friday 12th December
So unseasonably warm yesterday—15 degrees—there were small flies about, and green shoots in the garden.

Calm this morning so as planned we went over to the Lighthouse but there was a rising swell and the wind was forecast to go southerly and swell so we didn't linger. I cleaned the cottage while Ernest and Col. did the technical stuff in the tower. In one of the bedrooms, alongside greasy paperbacks (*Cowboy* by J. T. Edson and Sven Hassel's *Liquidate!*) an old Bible lies open at Revelation XX: 'And I saw the dead great and small stand before God . . . And the sea gave up the dead which were in it; and death and hell delivered up the dead which were in them: and they were judged every man according to his works. And whosoever was not found written in the Book of Life was cast into the Lake of Fire . . .' I try to imagine which of the engineers has found this comforting reading.

A short dark afternoon. I read a poetry collection for a review, enjoying evocations of light and heat in the Mediterranean. It was good on the Rhondda, too.

Tuesday 16th December
S.E. 5-7.
With Kim to Glyn-y-Weddw to recce for our Poetry and Painting course *Landscapes of the Imagination* next month. Whitecaps and swell, biting cold, bright and exhilarating. We walked down the lane through piles of beech leaves to Llanbedrog beach, (winter heliotrope in bud by the stream) then up to the headland of Western gorse and heather. Spectacular vistas of mountains—it was easy to imagine the peaks of Eryri as islands. Then back down a broad track through a small oak wood whistling in the wind and to Tŷ'n Gamdda for a cup of tea and to watch greenfinches feeding at the bird table a few feet from Kim's kitchen window. The India pictures are full of coppery heat and jungle.

Ernest had been to get a load of logs after hearing a forecast for blizzards and winds straight out of Siberia (record low temperatures in Moscow).

Wednesday 17th December
Bitterly cold (minus 10 windchill—the weatherpersons say). Too cold for Col. and Gwydion to carry on walling on Rhiw mountain.

Sat by a good fire writing cards that need time.

OAKS AT WINTER SOLSTICE
For Joan Hague

To each stretched finger
Snow has dressed the bare branches
In ghosts of summer.

187

Friday 19th December
Warm and sunny. Col. and Ernest over to the island with ten sacks of post and to 'give the generator a good seeing to'. (Tim phoned last night to say it had stopped—he's got ten newborn piglets under a lamp and about 200 lbs of pork in the freezer!)

I stayed home, boiling Christmas puddings—Nain's way, in a cloth.

Sunday 21st December
Winter solstice.
The sun broke through clouds this morning red as a plastic beach ball; but not much warmth in it. Ernest and Col. brought the last of the pots in. A few handfuls of big prawns in them—I dislike boiling them, though. They huddle together in the bucket as if protecting each other, and their eyes are in the top of their heads so they watch you as you lift the bucket to tip them into the boiling water. They die instantly, of course, and are spared any foreknowledge of it, but they certainly fear me as a predator.

Gillian Clarke's Christmas card arrived today. I kept it till last to open. Each year, a treasure: a photograph by David, a new poem by Gillian. This year, Lippizaner mares and their black foals and a wonderful poem about each young horse *shedding shadow from its skin / hair by hair until it is white as winter.*

In the week after Christmas I get the poem by heart and keep the cards to hand on the shelf where I write. There are eight now, lines which I hope to keep as long as my memory lasts.

Wednesday 24th December
Atlantic low moving very rapidly S.E. severe gale 9-10, perhaps violent storm 11.
Wind and rain from first light, but not unusually strong until after lunch when Ernest decided to go and secure the boat down in Porth Meudwy—big tides too, so he's already moved it behind the boathouse. I went down with him as far as the turning to Tŷ'n Gamdda, then walked on up with Christmas

presents, having to struggle to make headway against the wind. By 4 pm all the windows were trembling, the house seemed to shake with each new gust and telephone and the electricity were off. Col. reported slates and even wooden doors flying on the road from Rhiw.

Thursday 25th December
S.E. severe gale 9.
A dreadful night, but the wind has eased down a little. It seems strange after all that violent noise to look out on the same landscape. We have not heard yet how much damage there may be, or where, but we seem to have come through. The old caravan's wrecked, but that was due for clearing anyway. As soon as it was light, Ernest went down to check the boat.

We had our traditional walk after lunch. The tide was high up the beach; we stood for a time watching the wild white spray furiously smashing, pure energy as it meets the rock; drawing in its breath as if with rage as it falls back.

We are lucky to have the Rayburn to cook the turkey—it will probably be days before the power is back on, such a big area is affected. We have a fire to sit by, plenty of candles and no holes in our roof.

Saturday 27th December
S.E. 6-7.
Electricity and telephone came back on last night, and Linda rang to tell us Aberdaron had been on the front page of *The Times* with the highest winds of 111 mph. It was still windy but people are getting on with repairs quickly.

I noticed a few flowers on the escallonia. Snowdrop leaves growing strongly; daffodils and crocus are well up, but not showing flowerbuds yet.

Two walks today—up Anelog and along Whistling Sands beach just before dark. The sea still ragged, hurt-looking. It's roared itself hoarse.

For the first time in ten days, tonight the stars are visible.

Tuesday 30th December

A dark, wet and windy day, sunken, heavy, like 'the year's midnight' as John Donne wrote of St Lucy's Day, the twenty-first.

But there's a letter from Esther in Uganda, with a wonderful exuberant card she's drawn herself of women dancing under a bright orange sun. She writes of learning traditional medicine and pounding eucalyptus leaves for a cold—I must send her Menna Elfyn's poem about it, *ffiseg gwella annwyd*. She misses the sound of Welsh almost more than anything, she says. There's a photo of her standing by a waterfall in gorilla country. She's just eighteen, living on rice and a few beans, teaching English, Science and P.E. to a class of 58 9-13 year-olds, with little in the way of books or equipment; half her pupils have lost at least one parent to AIDS, and she's bright-faced, ready to tackle anything.

Wednesday 31st December

'Nine-tenths of our life is well forgotten in the living,' wrote William Carlos Williams. I suppose every year changes each of us, subtly, though we don't recognise how or why. I've had so much more time to discover things, birds, especially; I never really saw a wheatear before—their slanting flight, the way their stripes of silver and chocolate brown catch the light. I didn't consider it necessary to know the names of everything— that names are only the labels we put on things—but knowledge of the detail is a kind of honouring the pattern.

The fulmars are back; after four months silent wandering over thousands of miles in the Atlantic, long dark nights and their pituitary glands have prompted them back to the noisy cliff-ledge nest-sites, although they will not breed until May. And the lights are on in Wil Gwyddel's lambing shed at Gwagnoe. The cycle goes on.